MW00849912

TREASON

BY LIES, DECEPTION, AND FRAUD

TREASON

BY LIES, DECEPTION, AND FRAUD

MIKE BLACKWELL

SOVEREIGN PRESS
Denton, Texas

TREASON

Copyright © 2019 by Mike Blackwell

All rights reserved. No part of this book may be reproduced in any form or by any means—whether electronic, digital, mechanical, or otherwise—without permission in writing from the publisher, except by a reviewer, who may quote brief passages in a review.

All Scripture quotations from the New King James Version®. Copyright © 1982 by Thomas Nelson. Used by permission. All rights reserved.

Published by
Sovereign Press
Denton, Texas

www.sovereignpress.net

Library of Congress Control Number: 2019930775

Paperback ISBN: 978-1-949021-47-9
eBook ISBN: 978-1-949021-48-6

Printed in the United States of America

To God's children and to the American patriots who are seeking Truth, God, revival, and the restoration of this great country

CONTENTS

PREFACE

This book is dedicated to the God of Abraham, Isaac and Jacob. The God revealed in the Bible. The God of TRUTH and RIGHTOUSNESS. To God's children and to the American patriots who are seeking Truth, God, revival and the restoration of this Great country and its Constitutional Republic.

I give thanks and honor to America's veterans. Especially the Vietnam veterans and the men of the 5th Special Forces Group. I wish to thank the men of the 5th Special Forces Group, MACV SOG, for the privilege and honor in serving with them in the Republic of South Vietnam.

Through my experiences, I learned the value of our freedom and liberty as defined in our founding documents. As time goes by, I realize the importance of my oath of office to defend the constitution of the United States of America against all enemies, foreign and domestic. I realized the price of freedom and liberty paid for in blood and treasure by our forefathers and those that have followed them through the generations.

I realize that freedom and liberty is rare and fragile. It has to be defended by every generation otherwise they will be lost. We are at a crossroads in history. This is one of the reasons I decided to write this book. For the physical and moral dangers are real to this great country called America. But there is a greater danger that has taken hold of America, and the exposure of this great danger to the American people is the other reason I am writing this book.

At first I was hesitant to write this book, but I believe that from the day in the jungles of Laos when I cried out to God to save me, I have been called to proclaim this message.

I have to confess, I have been an extremely slow learner. But God is patient, kind and merciful. I believe that I have been born for such a time of this. God has given me the experiences, understanding, and knowledge to find the truth. God has also given me the will and faith to write this book.

I wrote this book for one purpose: to tell the absolute truth to the best of my ability. What you will discover and hopefully begin to understand, that truth is not what we have been taught or what the media and the powers that be tell us. As the truth begins to bring light, the reader will begin to see that we are living in a reality fraught with lies, fraud, and evil. Many crimes have been committed against the trusting American people and the people of the rest of the world. In a sense, we have all been like innocent sheep being led to the slaughter by people we trust.

It is my hope, that the information and facts that I provide in these pages bring some knowledge and understanding to these areas that are discussed. To substantiate the information, my primary sources will be scripture from the Holy Bible, Supreme Court Cases from the United States Supreme Court, statutory law, federal regulations from various agencies and the Congressional Record.

In 1851 Pierre-Joseph Proudhon, the founder of mutualist philosophy and the first anarchist, wrote about an ideal society in which frontiers are abolished, national states eliminated, and authority decentralized. He said:

> To be governed is to be watched, inspected, spied upon, directed, law-driven, numbered, regulated, enrolled, indoctrinated, preached at, controlled, checked, estimated, valued, censured, commanded by creatures who have neither the right nor the wisdom and the virtue to do so. To be governed is to be at every operation, at every transaction, noted, registered, enrolled, taxed, stamped, measured, numbered, assessed, licensed, authorized, admonished, prevented, forbidden, reformed, corrected, punished. It is, under pretext of public utility, and in the name of the general interest, to be placed under contribution, trained, ransomed, exploited, monopolized, extorted from, squeezed, hoaxed, robbed; then, at the slightest resistance, the first word of complaint, to be repressed, fined, despised, harassed, tracked,

abused, clubbed, disarmed, bound, choked, imprisoned, judged, condemned, shot, deported, sacrificed, sold, betrayed: and, to crown all, mocked, ridiculed, outraged, dishonored. That is government; that is its justice; that is its morality."

America today has gradually become what Pierre-Joseph Proudhon describes above. Has this always been the case in American history? Not always, for in the past, Americans had freedom and liberty. This made America the destination of millions of people from all over the world, and they are still coming to America for the hope of freedom and liberty.

It is my belief that most people will see the light using common sense and most importantly, Divine Revelation. Once the treason, lies, deceit, and frauds are exposed, we can move towards a peaceful resolution of all the issues. I have great faith in the goodness and common sense of the American people to see the truth.

May the American people turn back to the God of the Bible and this country's founding documents quickly, for time is short.

> *"My people are destroyed for lack of that knowledge. Because you have rejected knowledge, I also will reject you from being a priest for Me; Because you have forgotten the law of your God, I also will forget your children"* **(Hosea 4:6).**

1

WAR AND SALVATION

I have been studying the basic betrayal of the Republic of South Vietnam by the UNITED STATES OF AMERICA by the powers that be and the consistent betrayal of our allies since the early 1970s when I came back from the Vietnam War. Veterans were treated horribly by the leftist college faculty members, students, the media, the government and the general public. What these brainwashed individuals said was not the truth. I know this because I was there in South Vietnam. It is the same pattern today. The powers that be, have replaced truth with lies. Back then, the studies seemed to lead in this direction, but I lacked the historical studies and proof which Anna von Reitz, an Alaskan common law judge, author, and American state national expert, and others have provided. Besides, it was just too farfetched, and I did not want to believe that there was such evil, fraud, deceit and lies involved in this conspiracy. After the war I was in the real estate business. I had many friends who were bankers, lawyers, and investors. I respected them and figured they all could not be wrong. So I continued in the system, trying to make a living and paying the bills.

I am a Christian, a child of the Most High God, the creator of the heavens and the earth. This God, my God, is described and shows himself in scripture in the Bible. I am sharing this with you, because I want to share my long journey from a young man graduating from high school believing in the American dream, John Wayne, mom, apple pie, the girl next door, honor, justice, and truth to a more mature individual with a realistic view of where we are today. In 1967 the Vietnam War was raging. I had spent a semester at a junior college and learned nothing. It was so easy, it was a joke. I decided I needed to grow up and enlist in the Army. I am patriotic. I love America, the constitution, and our way of life. My oldest brother, Rocky, was a medic in the Army Special Forces and served in South Vietnam from 1963 to 1965. He served on an A Team in the Tay Ninh province in South Vietnam. He and his friends were my heroes.

My brother Leigh was a great high school long distance runner in Texas and was one of the best in the state in 1965. After high school he went to college for a while and decided to marry his wife, Charlotte. Shortly after that, Leigh decided to join the Army and the Special Forces. It was very difficult back then. Only about three out of a hundred people ended up wearing the Green Beret. After thirty years of service, Leigh retired as a sergeant major. Over those years he served in the 10th, 1st, and 5th Special Forces Groups out of Okinawa, Japan, and Germany, and he trained foreign troops in many locations. Leigh became a master parachutist, scuba instructor, drill instructor, and had a great military career. Most important, he was a good husband and father. Leigh was my hero too.

Being competitive and patriotic, I basically had no choice but to follow in my brother's footsteps. I enlisted in October 1967 and reported for duty on February 1, 1968. I had the pleasure of basic training in Fort Polk, Louisiana, and volunteered for airborne infantry training in Fort Gordon, Georgia, followed by volunteering for jump school in Fort Benning, Georgia. The war was running hot at this time and many of my friends had already shipped out to the Republic of South Vietnam. I often wonder what happened to them. After jump school I volunteered for Special Forces training at Fort Bragg, North Carolina. The sergeants who greeted us were relaxed and very professional. It was quite a change from the previous training. But make no mistake, once training began, it was tough and challenging and many men did not make it to the end.

Upon graduation I was assigned to the 10th Special Forces Group in Bad Tolz, Germany. At that time, if a Special Forces soldier wanted his assignment changed, there was a woman in the Pentagon who you could call and make your request for a change in assignment. It was not guaranteed, but she would do her best to honor your request. I called her and asked for assignment to the 5th Special Forces Group in the Republic of South Vietnam. She asked why I didn't want to be in Germany, which was a choice assignment at the time. I explained that my brother Leigh was stationed in Fort Devens, Massachusetts with the 10th Special Forces Group. He was married and had two children. At that time, the military would not allow two brothers in a combat zone at the same time. I stated that I would rather go in harm's way, than Leigh since I was not married. She understood and told me to call her in a couple of days. When I called her back, she said that she could not get me into the 5th Special Forces Group in the Republic of South Vietnam, but she could get me to the 1st Special Forces Group in Okinawa, Japan. She said if I still choose to go to South Vietnam, it would be easier to volunteer from there.

In Okinawa I learned that the 1st Special Forces Group were sending men to South Vietnam for six months of TDY (temporary duty). The emphasis was on training to prepare for combat duty. While in Okinawa, I had the opportunity to train with SEAL Team Six for about a week as they were rotating from the states to South Vietnam. On their way they stopped to train with us and exchange information and tactics. They were very good. I volunteered for duty with the 5th Special Forces Group about the second week after my arrival to the 1st Special Forces Group. About nine months later I came back to the states on a thirty-day leave and then deployed to the Republic of South Vietnam.

When I arrived at Tan Son Nhut Airport in Saigon, South Vietnam, I was twenty years old, 170 pounds, in great shape, and highly motivated. At the processing center in Long Binh, South Vietnam I had a rude awakening. The processing clerk informed me that he was assigning me to a regular infantry unit. They desperately needed platoon sergeants. Apparently, General Abrams, the commanding general in South Vietnam at the time, hated Special Forces troops and gave orders to assign them to regular infantry units in order to solve the problem of a shortage of non-commissioned officers in those units. I informed the processing clerk that I had been training a long time and wanted to be assigned to a Special Forces unit. This was not a friendly exchange.

"Ok," he snapped back. "If you want to be assigned to a Special Forces unit, I can get you into one. But you have to volunteer for it, and it is basically a suicide mission."

Aggravated and obviously not having good sense, I said, "Sign me up."

The clerk laughed and said okay.

Shortly thereafter I flew to Nha Trang, South Vietnam, where the 5th Special Forces Group was headquartered. There I met Paul Kennecott, later code-named Snowbank. Kennecott had just arrived. He was from Alaska, and we fast became friends. We were then assigned to 5th Special Forces Group Special Operations Augmentation (SOA) at Command and Control Central or CCC. Shortly after arriving, we departed for Kontum in a C-123 cargo aircraft. Upon arrival, we were greeted at the dirt airstrip by a Special Forces soldier and driven to the base a couple of miles away.

To my surprise, the sergeant major happened to be my old sergeant major from the 1st Special Forces group in Okinawa. There were three of us new guys, also known as fresh meat. The sergeant major explained that the mission was top secret. It was against the Geneva Convention of 1954. If we chose to continue, we needed to know that we would not be wearing US uniforms; we would not wear our dog tags or anything that identified us as Americans. We were to lead indigenous troops (Montangards) behind enemy lines. If captured, the American government would deny that we were American soldiers. He told us if we did not want to proceed, we should tell him now and he would reassign us. If we chose to go forward, he would disclose the rest of the information.

We all stated we wanted to proceed. The sergeant major then pulled the curtain back that was on a large wall in his office. Behind it, was a large map of South Vietnam, Cambodia, and Laos focusing on the tri-border area of the three countries. Our area of operations would focus on northern Cambodia, southern Laos all the way up to an area that was north of the DMZ (demilitarized zone) of North and South Vietnam. He stated that CCN area of operations were North Vietnam and Northern Laos, and CCS was central and southern Cambodia. The sergeant major assigned me to the radio communications team in the TOC (tactical command center).

One of my first days working in the radio center at the TOC, Frank Miller's recon team came under heavy attack as they were infiltrating from South Vietnam into southern Laos. The North Vietnamese were pretty efficient in tracking our helicopter insertions, and many of the recon teams would come into heavy contact with the North Vietnamese troops shortly after being inserted. Frank wanted to try to walk into Laos from South Vietnam and thereby slip in unnoticed by the North Vietnamese. As they were traversing a small creek in Laos, one of the Montangnards tripped a booby trap, which exploded and wounded him badly. Others in the recon team were wounded with shrapnel.

The team bandaged the wounded and Frank moved them to higher ground. As the team was moving they came under attack. The team repelled the attack and continued to move to higher ground so that they would be in a better position to call in air strikes. Frank established commo (communications) with the Covey, a two-seater OV-10 aircraft whose job was to insure commo with recon teams. Normally there were not that many teams operating, and the Covey was available twice a day: once in the morning and once in the afternoon. One of our experienced sergeants in the Covey would communicate with the recon team and then call in air strikes when necessary.

Franks recon team was in deep trouble. A running gun battle ensued after the first attack as Frank tried to move his team to higher ground. By this time Frank was wounded in the arm, and it was useless. Everyone on Frank's team was wounded. Movement was slow. Frank was actually in the best condition compared to the rest of his team. Covey advised Frank that the North Vietnamese were trucking in troops from several directions, surrounding him and his team. When the air support arrived, the Covey started directing air strikes. The NVA (North Vietnamese Army) kept coming in greater numbers. The NVA were battle hardened infantry troops who were very good. They hated the American recon teams, and their commanders offered a ten-thousand-dollar bounty on each American captured or killed. The NVA troops were motivated and kept coming even as they took casualties from the air strikes and Frank's recon team.

After dragging or carrying his team to higher ground, Frank went back down and ambushed the approaching NVA troops. He had to fire his CAR-15 rifle with one arm, stopping only to throw grenades. He had to pull the pins with his teeth since one of his arms was useless. Frank then returned to his team and moved them to higher ground, repeating the process until finally the team could not move anymore. Everyone was badly wounded, and Frank was the last guy able to defend the team. The team was under constant attack. To avoid the air strikes, the NVA would get as close as possible to the recon team. The air support would not bomb for fear of accidently hitting Frank and his team. In the meantime, Frank kept firing his rifle and throwing grenades in an attempt to not be overrun.

Covey called for a Bright Light Team (a rescue force of Montangnards led by American Special Forces). The team that arrived to help Frank were inserted near Frank's team. The first seven or so men to hit the ground made it to Frank's location, but they were all killed or wounded in the first five minutes. The battle continued throughout the day with heavy airstrikes and casualties. Eventually Frank and his team were rescued. Everyone got out, including the dead and wounded.

Frank recovered from his wounds and returned to running missions. He had been in South Vietnam for six years when I met him. He was a professional and was eventually awarded the Medal of Honor for his actions that day. I learned a lot from him. He befriended me and taught me. I am thankful.

Being fresh meat, hearing the commo and the firefight and the air strikes on the radio bothered me. It bothered me because I was safe in the TOC while good men were fighting and dying. After a couple of days of thinking about this, I informed the sergeant major that I wanted to be reassigned to the recon company.

Depending on the mission, recon teams ran mostly with six to nine men and were led by two to three

American's. The largest team I saw had fifteen men. They traveled light but were heavy on weapons and ammunition. Most missions were designed to last about seven to eight days. The missions varied, from monitoring the Ho Chi Minh Trail running through Laos and Cambodia to calling in air strikes on the truck conveys, tank parks and anti-aircraft positions protecting the trail to prisoner snatches for intelligence to assassinations. The most gratifying missions were rescuing pilots who were shot down. The assortments of missions were interesting.

The psyops missions were hilarious in a way. They were psychological operations designed to rattle the minds of the enemy. For example, once we dropped a couple of transistor radios along a heavily used trail so that they would be found by NVA soldiers. The radio could only get one radio station. The station was run by the CIA and broadcast news and information meant to demoralize the NVA troops. Another time teams dropped counterfeit NVA currency on various trails. This would help inflate their currency. Another operation was to sneak into an NVA area to plant defective ammo into their ammo supply. When they went to use the faulty mortar shells, they would blow up.

These were dangerous times and dangerous missions. It was an all-volunteer unit. If you did not want to run missions, you did not have to. The men were motivated, professional, and had a can-do attitude. It has been documented that our teams suffered a 200 percent casualty rate annually. We truly were dead men walking. These Special Forces soldiers still volunteered for the missions. In my opinion, they were America's finest, and I had the honor of serving among them. They were men who were short on talk but strong in action and courage. Our unit was finally awarded a Presidential Unit Citation for our services.

The sergeant major granted my request to be assigned to the recon company. I was assigned to Recon Team Hawaii (or RT Hawaii). The team leader (known as the one zero) was Sergeant First Class (SFC) John White, a very experienced soldier. Staff Sergeant (SSG) Terrance C. Spoon was the assistant team leader (the one one). Although he was on his first Vietnam tour, he was experienced too. (Later I was told he retired a lieutenant colonel.) I was the new guy (fresh meat, the one two).

The new guy carried the PRC-25 radio. It was heavy, about twenty-five pounds, and if a firefight ensued with the NVA, they targeted the radio operator. It made good sense for the NVA to kill the radio operator or destroy the radio. If they did, the rest of the team would be theirs since the recon team would be behind enemy lines, outnumbered, outgunned, and with no air support. As the new guy gained experience and competence, he would move up to the one one (assistant team leader) slot in the recon team and eventually to the one zero slot as recon team leader.

John White, Terrance Spoon, and the Montangnards welcomed me to the team. The Montangnards were tribes that lived in the tri-border area of Cambodia, Laos, and Vietnam. They did not like the Vietnamese, and the Vietnamese did not like them. The yards, as we called them, hated the communists and fought them for decades. They were great troops, brave and fearless. They lived in the mountains and jungles of the tri-border area of South Vietnam, Northern Cambodia and Southern Laos; were one with the environment; and loved the American's for helping them. It was an honor to serve with them and become their friends.

Training began in earnest. We ran immediate action drills if ambushed; drills to withdraw orderly, returning fire as the team retreated from a superior force; weapons familiarization; physical training; and just becoming familiar with the team members. While this was going on John White also had to prepare for our next mission that was assigned to the team. The recon team leader was responsible for gathering all available intelligence; doing an aerial flyover of the area of operations to become familiar with the terrain; and basically to plan the team's insertion point, extraction plan, and escape plan, if needed, to accomplish the mission given to the team from Saigon.

Orders came down for me to attend Recondo School south of Saigon. I went and trained and did well. Actually, I came in second in the class, which is something that I am proud of. The previous training helped, and this type of stuff came easily to me. I came back to Kontum and RT Hawaii and continued to train.

John White was having an ongoing health issue with a hernia that was bulging larger than a baseball. He was temporary removed from recon duty and Terrance Spoon took over as team leader on a temporary basis.

Recon Team Hawaii was assigned the mission to infiltrate an area overlooking the Ho Chi Minh Trail going through Laos. It was known as Hotel 6. Area of operations were in square grids, so many kilometers by so many kilometers, and were overlaid on large maps of Cambodia, Laos, and North Vietnam. If a team was operating in Hotel 6, General Abrams and his staff all new the exact location of the Recon Teams quickly and efficiently. Hotel 6 was heavily defended by battle-hardened NVA troops. The NVA had infantry patrols guarding the trail network, they had tank parks, and many anti-aircraft guns in the area. I remember being briefed on the area, and I remember they had about ten thousand troops in our small area of operations. At night, convoys of truck traffic passed through the heading towards Central and South Vietnam. The trail was actually a bunch of dirt roads that allowed the NVA to infiltrate troops and material into South Vietnam. This area was officially off limits for US troops. In reality, we were operating in the area, and many air strikes were hitting the NVA. It was not enough to stop them, but it did hurt their war effort against the South Vietnamese.

General Abrams and his staff wanted intelligence on enemy strength, equipment, and movement of troops and supplies. Therefore, the missions were assigned to us out of Saigon. Three previous teams had been assigned to Hotel 6 to gather intelligence. The goal was to monitor the trail as long as possible, and when ready to leave, we were to call in air strikes. The average length of a mission was to be about a week to ten days. The three previous teams did not last more than six hours each on the ground. They were all shot up with dead and wounded. This was a very hot dangerous location, and the NVA did not want us there.

We left Kontum by helicopter to Dak To, our launch site into Laos. There was a helicopter company assigned to us out of Pleiku whose responsibility was to insert and extract the teams. They were the best. They were young, professional and courageous. We loved these guys.

RT Hawaii was inserted mid-morning on a beautiful day of blue skies with a few white soft clouds overhead. The insertion site was selected by the Team Leader (known as the 10) Staff Sergeant Terrance C. Spoon. I was carrying the PRC-25 radio and serving in the role of the assistant team leader. There were four yards accompanying us. One was a Kit Carson Scout, he was a former NVA soldier who changed sides. He was very good. He hated the communists, loved to go on missions and kill them. He was aggressive, smart and loved John Wayne movies and American Levi's. He was very brave. Actually, the other three yards were great also, just different personalities. They all loved American Special Forces soldiers. We loved them also.

As mentioned earlier, we inserted into Hotel 6, this was our area of operations. Anyone who served there will tell you, this was a hot target. After the insertion, we moved very slowly and quietly, with the team's last man covering and brushing away our tracks so the team would avoid detection. We methodically moved along the middle of the mountains, avoiding the valley where water was and the NVA would congregate and the ridge lines where the NVA traveled on foot. There were major foot trails that NVA troops used on a regular basis to travel quickly on the ridge lines. The terrain was mountainous and heavily foliaged. You could hear the animals in the jungle noticing our quiet passage through their kingdom. The monkeys were playing in the high tree tops, about one hundred feet above us in the jungle canopy, the parrots and other birds were chirping.

We had a problem. It was standard operating procedure for the NVA to monitor all the insertion points with trackers who were very good. They would see the general area where the team was inserted and then would make their way to the insertion point, pick up the trail, and track the team. We had picked up two trackers. As we quietly made our way through the heavy jungle and forest towards the Ho Chi Minh Trail, the trackers were on our left and right rear, signally our direction via a gunshot in the jungle about every hour or so to notify other NVA troops in the area of our location so they could converge on RT Hawaii and to take out the six-man team. I do not know if the trackers were equipped with any type of radio or had a runner to notify their headquarters or not. I do know they were on our trail, and we were having difficulty losing them.

About every hour, there would be a locating shot from each tracker. The cat and mouse games continued into the third day, as we continually made our way closer to a location where we could monitor the trail. At about eleven in the morning of the third day we were crossing a trail on a ridgeline. First the point man, a yard, and the one zero (Terrance Spoon) crossed the crest of the ridgeline and started descending into the heavy foliage. Then another two yards crossed the crest of the ridgeline. The American carrying the radio was the key to the trap. That was me. Suddenly, a massive amount of AK-47 automatic weapon fire exploded. I grabbed the mic of the PRC-25, which was attached to my combat harness on my left chest, squeezed it, and yelled, "Contact, Contact!" The next second, there was a loud explosion, and I was thrown into the air before tumbling to the ground, landing in a thicket of wait-a-minute vines. Bullets were hitting all around me. I was dazed and struggling to get free from the vines. Out of the corner of my eye, I see the tail gunner, my Montangnard friend, standing in the center of the trail giving return fire to the ambushers. He looked like John Wayne with bullets hitting all around him. This gave me enough time to get free, and then we sprinted with all our gear and weapons down the slope with the NVA fast on our tail. The rest of our team took off, but they were waiting to see if we were coming or not. We joined up and took off. The chase was on.

We were deep into Laos on a secret mission not wearing US Army uniforms and without any identification. We had quite a few NVA chasing us, and we knew the NVA was setting up a blocking force to finish us off. We were out of radio contact because we were descending the mountain and radio communication was rare. Normally, it just happened twice a day, when Covey (the OV-10) flew over in the morning to get our sit rep (situation report) and then in the late afternoon or early evening. We had already talked to the Covey earlier in the morning, and they flew over only twice a day. The next scheduled contact with him was to be late in the afternoon, and without air support, we were in deep trouble. The afternoon was too late.

To my surprise and joy, about an hour later Covey came on the radio asking if we were okay. This never happens. Covey usually only checked on teams in the morning and near dusk, weather permitting. Apparently, a CIA radio relay site deep in Laos on the top of a high mountain heard my brief communication yelling "Contact, Contact" and the AK-47 fire and the explosion. They contacted Covey and told him one of his teams was in trouble. SSG Spoon took the radio and started carrying it and communicating with Covey, explaining the situation. Covey called in air support and started looking for an extraction point for us.

As the A1-E Spads and other fighters arrived on station, Covey directed the air strikes like a maestro. This continued for seven long hours as Covey gave SSG Spoon directions to a small clearing in the heavy jungle and forest canopy where a chopper could lower a rope ladder to the team for extraction. It was a long way off, and we had to get there before dusk. Missing the extraction would mean certain capture, which was not an option since the NVA gave no quarter to the recon teams. They hated us for going into Laos and Cambodia and causing havoc in their rear areas. Capture was a fate worse than death.

In fact, America abandoned many of the American pilots and Special Forces soldiers who had been captured in Laos and Cambodia when they signed the peace agreement with the North Vietnamese and obtained the release of some of the American prisoners captured in North Vietnam. The North Vietnamese did not release all the Americans. This was and is a national disgrace. I am disgusted with Henry Kissinger, Richard Nixon, and the American government for abandoning these men. It makes me sick. To be fair, we were told if we were captured, the U.S. government would not acknowledge us and we would be abandoned. We volunteered anyway. The U.S. Military and our fellow soldiers in arms would never abandon us. Now, politicians, that is another matter as history teaches us. It still makes me sick.

As we continued to go up and down the high

mountains attempting to escape from the NVA who were massing in the area, SSG Spoon and Covey continued the coordination of the air strikes as we attempted to escape. The problem was there were too many NVA troops in our area and we had to get the extraction point before dark. We were running behind schedule and were tiring. Around four in the afternoon as we crossed a ridgeline, we took a break at a junction of trails. Each of us covered one of the trails in case enemy soldiers came upon us. We were all tired after four to five hours of being chased up and down the mountains. I rested my back and rucksack against a very large tree, facing one of the trails. I made no effort to protect myself. Breathing heavily, I just waited for the NVA to come up the trail. I was done running. I simply wanted to kill some NVA and meet my fate.

As I sat there, I said to God, "God, if you get me out of here and save me, I will serve you the rest of my days." To this day I have no idea where that thought came from. I was clueless about the Bible and God's Word.

Our break lasted about fifteen minutes. During that time, Covey and SSG Spoon discussed our situation. They determined we were not going to make it to the extraction point before dusk. If that was true, we would be dead by morning. So we discussed it and decided to run the ridge lines using the NVA trails. It would save us a lot of time. The only danger was running into an NVA patrol searching for us. It was a chance we decided to take.

For the next two to three hours we ran the ridge line

trails. The sun was setting and dusk was upon us when we reached the extraction point. Covey had coordinated our extraction with the Huey choppers and the Cobra gunships. The gunships prepped the extraction site with heavy gunfire and the Huey came in and dropped the rope ladder. Two of the yards went up the rope latter first and then I was next. I barely made it up to the chopper, and the door gunner grabbed my web gear and pulled me in. The other two yards came up and then SSG Spoon. We lifted up and away from the extraction point. We gained altitude, and finally we were safe.

What a day! What an adrenaline rush! The door gunners were great to us and the cool air at about four thousand feet washed away the stress and heat from our bodies. The chopper crew gave us fresh pineapple slices as we flew back to Dak To, South Vietnam, on a beautiful day with fluffy white clouds scattered amongst the blue sky. It was a great day to be alive!

We arrived at Dak To and then were flown back to Kontum by the Huey's and accompanied by the Cobra gunships. When we touched down at the camp chopper landing zone, it seemed like the entire camp was there to welcome us. Apparently they were listening to this from the radio communications of the Covey and the TOC (Tactical Operations Center). We were grabbed, hugged, patted on the back, congratulated on being alive, given cold beer as we made our way to our debriefing.

After the debriefing, we had seven days off. We could

stay in camp or go anywhere in South Vietnam. When we finished the time off, we would be assigned another mission and start preparing for it.

That was my first mission across the fence. The missions continued. The war, continued. Let me state clearly, I did no more than any other of my friends who were running missions across the fence during my tour. And I am sure that I did a lot less than many. I simply did the job that I volunteered to do, and I had the opportunity to serve with some real heroes, such as John Plaster, Frank Miller, John White, Terrance C. Spoon, Paul Kennecott, John Good, Pat Lucas, and many others. This story is told because it had a real impact on me. Part of it was reality set in. And the other part, and the main part, is I started on a life-long spiritual journey which continues to this day. I have also told this story to establish the fact that I do have a right to talk about Treason and the spiritual journey I have been on since that day.

2

AMERICA'S LAW

America has a great history, a history of hope. The God of the Bible has been involved in this great nation since the beginning, and that history is not taught in our schools, colleges, or universities. Our form of government is not taught in our schools, colleges, or universities. Why?

God's hand has always been on this great, vast land. God has preserved this land for his purposes. Eventually, God directed the first immigrants to come to America at Plymouth Rock. These people fled Europe for religious freedom. Many died in the first year, but they persisted in faith. More and more immigrants fled Europe for the sake of religious freedom. America began to grow. Most of the immigrants spoke English and believed the Bible to be the Word of God. As time went on, the new Americans first made farms out of the wilderness, and then they began to make cities. As they prospered, they gave thanks and worshiped God—the God of the Bible.

As more immigrants came to America, if they did not believe in the God of the Bible, that was okay. Individuals had the choice to worship as they chose. However, the vast majority of the new Americans were English, or European, and they were Bible believing individuals. As the colonies grew, naturally, they needed laws to govern them. All forms of law come from religion because religion establishes what is right and wrong. All authority comes from God. God gave the first man, Adam, authority over the earth. Later, Adam and the first woman, Eve, sinned. God gave Jesus, the Christ, all authority. Jesus Christ did not sin. Before Jesus left this earth, he gave all authority to the church. The law of the land in the Western World is based on the Mosaic law of the Bible, which is common to Judaism, Christianity, and Islam. The Ten Commandments are the basis of the law of the land, which in this country is American common law. The US Constitution is also formed under common law and is called the law of the land.[1]

In England in the 1600s people had legal right and title to the land. As the thirteen British colonies in America developed and grew, people had legal right and title to land, including the land in the West. In this way American common law is similar to British common law.

In the 1700s England was involved in many wars around the globe protecting its empire. They fought the War of the Spanish Succession (1701–1714), the War of the Austrian Succession (1740), the Carnatic Wars in

India (1744–1763), the Seven Years' War (1754–1763), and the American Revolutionary War (1775–1783), among others. These wars caused major financial stress for England, and as a consequence they increased the taxes and tariffs in the American colonies and sent a hoard of tax collector's and troops to the American colonies to collect the monies to fund England's global empire. As taxes and regulations increased and English agents and troops increased, American colonists became increasingly resistant.

American preachers and pastors discussed the situation of oppression and tyranny by England against the American colonies in their sermons and writings. Statesman and printer Benjamin Franklin spoke of these things in his publications and speeches. Thomas Paine, an American political activist and philosopher, did the same. There were many who spoke out against these evils. As resistance grew, the English applied more taxes and regulations.

When the taxes on tea (the most popular drink at the time) got too high, Founding Father Samuel Adams and others protested by throwing more than three hundred chests of British tea into the Boston harbor. This so-called Boston Tea Party helped crystalize the thinking of the American colonist. Unrest grew. Secret meetings were held and resistance flourished. The British continued trying to suppress the people. Patriot's like Patrick Henry, who declared "Give me liberty or give me death" in the Virginia legislature, rallied people to the cause of freedom. The beginnings of rebellion against the British continued to grow. These colonists were God-fearing men and women who abided by God's Word. They were not the kind of people who were rebellious for rebelliousness sake. But as they studied and discussed the issues, as they listened to their preachers and pastors, as they studied the Word of God, they yearned for freedom in their hearts. They trusted God. They had faith in God's Word. They knew that God said:

> The steps of a good man are ordered by the Lord; And he delights in his way. (Psalms 37:23)

> A man's steps are of the Lord; How then can a man understand his own way? (Proverbs 20:24)

> Your ears will hear a word behind you, saying, "This is the way, walk in it," Whenever you turn to the right hand Or whenever you turn to the left. (Isaiah 30:21)

> Trust in the Lord with all your heart and lean not upon your own understanding; In all your ways acknowledge him, And He shall direct your paths. (Proverbs 3:5-6)

> God is our refuge and strength, A very present help in trouble. Therefore, we will not fear, Even though

the earth be removed, And though the mountains carried into the midst of the sea. (Psalm 46:1-2)

Blessed is the man who makes the Lord his trust, And does not respect the proud, nor such as turn aside to lies. (Psalm 40:4)

Have I not commanded you? Be strong and take courage; do not be afraid nor be dismayed, for the Lord your God is with you wherever you go. (Joshua 1:9)

The American colonists had no choice but to organize in their individual legislatures and begin the move to liberty. God had a divine plan for America. Eventually, in 1775, the First Continental Congress met in Philadelphia, Pennsylvania. Through much debate, anguish, soul searching, prayer, and negotiations, finally, on July 4, 1776, they declared independence. They voted for liberty, and essentially for war with the greatest military power on earth. They did this in Faith, trusting in Divine Providence, the Word of God, and the almighty God and creator of the universe. These men and women, our forefathers and their families, were bold, and trusted God and the truth. I am thankful and give honor to them who had the courage to stand on their convictions and the Word of God. I am proud to be an American.

The rest is history. But who's history? The history being taught in grammar and high school? The history they teach in the colleges and universities today? The history I learned in school made me proud to be an American. The schools have not been teaching that history for decades. Today in American schools, students are taught that America is the problem. Today our children are taught that America is racist, greedy, evil, and the source of all the world's problems. Today in American schools, the God of the Bible is not allowed. Really? They teach that America was created by wealthy racists, arrogant white men who designed our form of government to benefit a select few. Really? Is that true?

No, that is not true. America was created so that each man or woman, regardless of race and station in life would be the same as King George of England at the time. Do you know what that means? Most Americans do not. The reason is that they have been educated in public schools and are influenced by the media and the powers that be. Most Americans today believe the federal government is in control, and we the people have to obey it. We have to obey the IRS, the State Department, the US Treasury, the FBI, and all other government agencies. They all have authority over us. Really? Is that what the Declaration of Independence, the Constitution, and the Bill of Rights say? Do we have to obey the law? Absolutely! But the question is, what law do we have to obey?

America has two laws: the American common law and the UNTIED STATES statutory law. The question we should be asking is which law are we governed by? Do you know?

The American common law is the law of all of our founding documents. Any law that conflicts with the original US Constitution is null and void. The original Constitution is the supreme law of the land. The American nationals have a right to American common law. These government agencies, however, operate on statutory law and rules and regulations. Why is that? What is Statutory Law?

Statutory law is man-made law. It is written law or laws that are made up by legislative bodies to impose the will of corporate STATE upon its corporate CITIZENS. There are more statutory laws than anyone can count.

Therefore, it is extremely important to know our American history. Our history, and our choices today, allows us to have a political status of a slave, or like King George of England, a sovereign. What status would you like to have? What does the Bible say about Freedom and Liberty?

The authority of the United States is the Constitution. The US Constitution is the supreme law of the land, and any statute to be valid must be in agreement. It is impossible for both the Constitution and a law violating it to be valid. One must prevail. Any statute violating the Constitution is void and of no effect.

- "The Federal and State Governments are in fact but different agents and trustees of the people...the adversaries of the Constitution seem to have lost sight of the people altogether. They must be told that the ultimate authority resides in the people." (Federalist, no. 46 by James Madison)

- "No legislative act contrary to the Constitution can be valid. To deny this would be to affirm that the deputy is greater than his principle, that the servant is above the master; that the representatives of the people are superior to the people, that men, acting by virtue of powers, may do not only what their powers do not authorize, but what they forbid. . . . It is not otherwise to be supposed that the Constitution could intend to enable the representatives of the people to substitute their WILL in that of their constituents. . . . A Constitution is, in fact, and must be regarded by Judges as a fundamental law. . . . If there should happen to be an irreconcilable variance between the two, the Constitution is to be preferred to the statute." (Federalist, no. 78 by Alexander Hamilton)

- "The general rule is that an unconstitutional statute, though having the form and name of law, is in reality no law, but is wholly void and ineffective for any purpose; since unconstitutionality dates from the time of its enactment and not merely from the date of the decision so branding it; an unconstitutional law, in legal contemplation, is as inoperative as if it had never been passed . . . an unconstitutional law is VOID . . . it imposes no duty, converse no rights, creates no office, bestows no power or authority on anyone, affords no protection and justifies no acts performed under it . . . an unconstitutional law cannot repeal or supercede any existing valid law . . . an unconstitutional statue cannot repeal or in any way effect an existing one . . . the general principal stated above applied to the constitution as well as the laws of the several states insofar as they are repugnant to the constitution of the United States. (Marbury v. Madison: 5 US 137, 1803)
- "Neither the legislative, executive nor judicial departments of the Government can lawfully exercise any authority beyond the limits marked out by the Constitution."

(Dred Scott v. Sandford, 60 U.S. 393, 1857)

- "Daniel Webster, James Otis and Sir Edward Coke all pointed out that the mere fact of enactment does not and cannot raise statutes to the standing of LAW. Not everything which may pass under the form of statutory enactment can be considered the LAW of the land." (16 Am Jur, 2nd Sec. 547)

- "An act of legislation repugnant to the Constitution is void . . . for I cannot call it law contrary to the first great principles of the social compact . . . (It) cannot be considered a rightful exercise of legislative authority." (Calder v. Bull, 3 U.S. [3 Dall.] 386, 1798)

- "An unconstitutional statute, whether Federal or State, though having the form and name of law, is in reality no law, but is wholly null and void and ineffective for any purpose. . . . It imposes no duty, confers no rights, creates no office, bestows no power or authority on anyone, affords no protection and justifies no acts performed under it. . . . No one is bound to obey an unconstitutional act statute. No courts are bound to enforce it." (16 Am Jur, 2nd Sec. 256)

- "Where rights secured by the Constitution are involved, there can be no rule-making or legislation which would abrogate them." (Maranda vs State of Arizona, 86 S. Ct., 1602, 1966)

3

THE RIGHT TO DRIVE

We all know that we need a driver's license from the DMV (Department of Motor Vehicles) right? Since this is common knowledge, why does the Supreme Court say we do not? Here is some case law.

- "The right of a citizen to travel upon the public highways and to transport his property thereon, by horse-drawn carriage, wagon or automobile, is not a mere privilege which may be permitted or prohibited at will, but a common right which he has under his right to life, liberty and the pursuit of happiness. Under this constitutional guaranty one may, therefore, under normal conditions, travel at his inclination along the public highways or in public places, and while conducting himself in an orderly and decent manner, neither interfering with nor disturbing another's rights, he will be protected, not only in his person, but in his safe conduct." (Thompson v Smith, 154 SE 579, 11 American Jurisprudence Constitutional Law, section 329, page 1135)

- "The right of a Citizen to travel upon the public highways and to transport his property thereon, in the ordinary course of life and business, is a common right which he has under the right to enjoy life and liberty, to acquire and possess property, and to pursue happiness and safety. It includes the right, in so doing, to use the ordinary and usual conveyances of the day, and under the existing modes of travel, includes the right to drive a horse drawn carriage or wagon thereon or to operate an automobile thereon, for the usual and ordinary purpose of life and business." (W. L. Thompson v. D. C. Smith, Chief of Police, 155 Va. 367, 1930)

- "The use of the automobile as a necessary adjunct to the earning of a livelihood in modern life requires us in the interest of realism to conclude that the RIGHT to use an automobile on the public highways partakes of the nature of a liberty within the meaning of the Constitutional guarantees of which the citizen may not be deprived without due process of law. " (Berberian v. Lussier 139 A2d 869, 1958); See also: Schecter v. Killingsworth, 380 P.2d 136, 140; 93 Ariz. 273, 1963)

(For more court cases confirming that American Nationals do not need a driver's license please refer to appendix A.)

For most of us, we have been taught differently. Why is that? We trust our schools, colleges and universities to teach us the truth. We trust the media to report the truth. We trust our government to tell us the truth and operate in truth. We trust that American culture embraces the truth. So, why is there a conflict? Maybe we should continue to study and to seek the truth. Obviously there is a conflict between what we have been taught in school and case law since the founding of this country. Why?

We live in an age of deception, and a lot of our problems come from the members of the BAR Association. BAR stands for the British Accredited Registry. The members of the BAR do not practice American law as defined by the Constitution of 1787 and our other founding documents. No, they practice a private copywritten law owned by the Vatican. Why is that?

Why is it the members of the BAR (British Accredited Registry) have their own dictionary? It is called the Black's Law Dictionary. Why do they not use a Webster's dictionary or some other one? Well, the simple reason is they change the definitions of words to deceive the general public. A prime example is the phrase "United States." The vast majority of the American people will think this is the geographical land area of the combined fifty states. It is not. In lawyer legalese it is the ten square miles known as the District of Columbia and its territories. This is simply an example of their deceit against the American people and other people of the nations on planet earth.

Requiring a driver's license is an example of the deceit. It's time we wake up to that reality and to wake up to what has happened and is happening to your freedoms. There is something seriously wrong in America, and we need to understand it.

As I mentioned to obtain a driver's license a man or woman goes to the DMV—an agency or corporation of the state—in their home state. What happens? You apply for a driver's license from the DMV. The DMV is an agency/corporation of the state. In my case I live in Texas. So, the DMV is an agency/corporation of the STATE OF TEXAS. If you pass the tests required by the DMV, they will issue a license. This license gives you the privilege to drive. If you disobey the rules or regulations of the DMV, they will revoke your license, and, in some cases, they may fine or imprison you. Yet, according to the Constitution and case law we have the right to travel the highways and byways of this great country. It is indisputable as proven by the case law I referenced above and the case law in appendix A. Therefore, if you reclaim your political status as a free man or woman, you do not need a driver's license to travel the highways and byways of this great land.

For more than ten years I was a licensed real estate agent and broker. I did very well in the residential and commercial real estate markets. As I was slowly waking up to the law and how things worked, I wondered why I needed a license to make a living. I thought the constitution gave me the right to make a living. You can look at any profession today, you probably need a license to make your living. Why is that? Maybe we need to read our founding documents of this great country. They are the Declaration of Independence, the Constitution and the Bill of Rights.

When anyone applies for anything, you are asking permission to do a certain thing from your superior or master. You are the slave asking permission from the master. Most things we do in America today, we are applying for something. When you apply for something, there are terms and conditions you agree to. These terms and conditions limit your rights and freedoms and define who you are as it relates to the contract in which you are entering. If you are not wise, you will limit your freedoms and liberties when you enter into contracts.

When are forefathers won the Revolutionary War against the British and signed the Treaty of Paris (1783) and the Treaty of Versailles (1783), did they negotiate a slavery status for us against the defeated British?

No, they negotiated our freedoms and liberties because our forefathers were the victors. You need to read the Treaty of Versailles 1783 and the Treaty of Paris 1783.

Considering the freedoms that the founders fought so hard to obtain, why do we have to ask permission from some entity to pursue our livelihoods? Why are there so many government agencies that regulate virtually everything we do? Please show me the authority that these faceless entities have to do the things they do. And yes, they do have legal authority. The legal authority is derived from some statute in the statutory law under which they operate. Statutory law is not American common law, as we have seen.

Legal authority is not lawful authority. Legal authority is related to statutory law—the law of men. Lawful authority is related to common law, which is related to natural law or God's law.

Which law do you operate in? Which law do you have to obey? What are the consequences of obeying statutory law and not natural law or God's law? What are the consequences of obeying God's law and not statutory law? Can you do both? These questions have real answers and real consequences. Maybe you should know the answers to these questions.

4

A STORY OF AN
UNDERCOVER FBI AGENT

The year was 1979. My brother Rocky and I were in the apartment business in Texas. We bought old rundown apartments, rehabbed them, and then rented them. Our friends and family were investors. My brother's mother-in-law, Marga, lived in southern California and had been in the real estate business for a long time. She flew out to meet us with a friend of hers, a private investigator who happened to have the contract with LAX to provide security to the airport, to discuss possibly investing in our apartment rehab projects.

During dinner, after the normal niceties, he asked Rocky and me what our background was before getting into the real estate business.

Rock stated he had served in the Army in South Vietnam as a Special Forces medic on a Special Forces A Team between 1963 and 1965. After that he worked on offshore oil rigs in Borneo and the Caribbean. I told him about my service with the 5th Special Forces Group as part of MACVSOG from 1969 to 1970. Then I explained how I worked in the South Pacific for a government contractor as an A&P Mechanic where I met some great people from Air America, which was a CIA operation in the Vietnam War years, and other veterans. We told him we did our first apartment rehab deal in 1977.

He asked what we thought about the current political situation. Rock and I both are direct, so we told him flat-out we both thought it was disgraceful how the US Congress cut off funding to the South Vietnamese military in 1975, which caused the complete defeat of the South Vietnamese by the Communists a few months later. The Communist victory led to millions of our allies being murdered or imprisoned in brutal labor camps. The US Congress was either completely stupid, complicit, or corrupt, or all three.

Then I launched into what I thought of the news media. I explained to Marga's friend the news media was absolutely corrupt and did not report the truth to the American people and the world about what was happening in the Vietnam War. It was a propaganda tool of the communists, socialists, leftist, and others, who wanted to destroy America by manipulating American perception of the events. I told him how the New World Order boys used (and still are using) the media basically as a propaganda tool to further their agenda, which is the destruction of America and its form of government. They need to do this to merge America into their New World Order. This world government will be of a socialist-communist nature. Rock supported my contention with his own stories of a young Dan Rather in South Vietnam. Like the time Dan Rather showed up at Rock's Special Forces camp early one morning. This camp was operated by a Special Forces A Team which consisted of two officers and ten enlisted men. Rock was the Special Forces medic for the team, and their Vietnamese troops and their Chinese Nung mercenaries.

About mid-morning, Rock and most of the A team were in their tactical operation center (TOC) when there was an eruption of a massive amount of gunfire and the team thought they were under attack by the Viet Cong. As the team rushed out of the TOC to their defensive positions around the camp they discovered the source of the gunfire.

The young Dan Rather, in search of boosting his career had hired the Chinese Nung mercenaries and the Vietnamese troops to fake a battle so Dan Rather could be in the midst of a major battle giving the news and his camera crew is filming this great battle.

This was the beginning of Rock's disillusion with the media. As the years rolled by, Dan Rather became the famous television news reporter that presented the nightly news.

Rock's mother in law was absolutely horrified at this discussion. She made every effort to turn the conversation back to business and the weather. Unfortunately for Marga, this piqued Marga's friend and investor's interest. The conversation continued and then he disclosed something about his background that even Marga did not know.

As a young man, Marga's friend was recruited by the FBI to infiltrate the Communist cell operating in Hollywood, California. This was in the early 1950s during the famous Joe McCarthy era during which Senator McCarthy held hearings in Congress about the infiltration of Communists in the government.

The Communist cell was led by a single woman. At the time Marga's friend was young, fit, and good looking. The plan was for him to join the cell, get close the woman who was leading it, and gather intelligence for the FBI. And that's just what he did. For two years he was the leader's boyfriend. At that dinner he explained to us what he reported to the FBI. The communists had a forty-year plan to take over America through deception and infiltration from within. That was in the early 1950s, so their plan was to be complete by the early 1990s. Here are some of the points of the plan as he told us:

- to infiltrate the education system of America—from grammar school to universities— and teach socialism, which is very close to communism, in a favorable light;

- to infiltrate the seminaries of America;
- to infiltrate each states legislature and state agencies and eventually the governorships;
- to infiltrate the US Congress and their staffs;
- to infiltrate all the federal agencies and promote heavy government regulation and rules;
- to promote socialist and Communist legislation in Congress;
- to infiltrate the US military;
- to infiltrate all intelligence agencies;
- to pass legislation that causes a graduated tax system that destroys incentive and capitalism;
- to gradually destroy the currency of America by printing money and creating a massive national debt which cannot be paid back.

Cornel Herlong

Basically this is the Communist agenda as reported in the 1958 book the *Naked Communist* by Cleon Skousen and confirmed by Congressman Albert S. Herlong Jr. of Florida. On January 10, 1963, Congressman Herlong read the Communist agenda into the Congressional Record. (You can read the transcript in appendix B.)

It is interesting to note that one of the points was to infiltrate the seminaries. They know America's strength and unique character is that it is a Christian nation. It was founded on Christian principles that are expressed throughout the founding documents. The Communists knew if they could infiltrate the seminaries and water down the Word of God, America in time would cease to be a Christian nation, and when a nation ceases to be a nation of godly people it ceases to be a blessed nation. In *No* fact, it becomes a nation judged by God. The Communists knew that if this happens eventually America would fail. It will be judged by God like every other nation described in the Bible.

Looking back at history and then looking at today, does any of this look familiar? It is probably just coincidence. Or, could it be this plan is being executed, and the American people have been put to sleep by the main stream media, the majority of preachers today, and the dreadful education system?

I believe this is their plan. They are just running twenty to thirty years late due to the election of Ronald Reagan in 1980. Ronald Reagan bought America time. But America's enemy's plan basically did not change. They are patient and think strategically long term.

When Obama was running for President, he said that "he is the one that they have been waiting for." He was speaking to the leftists, socialists-communists, and the Islamic community. Throughout his administration he followed the Communist playbook. He made great progress but did not finish the job. He needed Hillary

Clinton to be elected president to complete the task of moving America into an irreversible socialist-communist Islamic paradise while the American people slept.

Then a strange thing happened, President Donald J. Trump won the election with the goal of making America great again. The media, the leftists, socialist-communists, New World Order people have gone ballistic. They had the prize in their hand, but the American people are beginning to wake up and understand the facts and the real dangers that we all face as the American people.

5

THE BIRTH CERTIFICATE FRAUD

Do you write your name in upper and lowercase letters? For example, my name is Michael Blackwell. My guess is that you write your name in upper and lowercase letters like I do. If that is the case, why is your name on your driver's license written in all capital letters like this: MICHAEL BLACKWELL?

Let's take a look at your social security card. Is your name in upper and lowercase, or is it written in all capital letters? It's written in all capitals. Why?

How about your Passport? Is your name in upper and lowercase or in all capitals? Why?

How about your name on your bank or brokerage account? Is it upper and lowercase or in all capital letters? Why?

How about every credit card you have? Is your name in upper and lowercase or in all capitals? Why?

If you ever have been sued, is your name upper and lowercase or all capitals? Why?

Look at any bill (invoice) that you have, is your name is all capital letters? Why?

Why does this even matter? Does this make any difference?

Do the attorneys and bankers know something we do not?

All of these state and federal agencies, do they know something we do not?

The answer is yes; capitalization does matter. It matters legally and lawfully. And yes, these people do know something we do not. Maybe mid-management does not know, but the higher-ups know it matters. It is their job to know. For the system is designed this way.

It matters because it legally confirms that you are a citizen of the United States of America. This is why the government agencies and commercial businesses open business accounts and banking accounts using all capital letters when writing your name. We all know that we are UNITED STATES citizens, right? No problem then.

So, what is the legal definition of the United States?

According to Title 28, United States Code § 3002 – Definitions

> (15) "United States" means –
> (A) a federal corporation;
> (B) an agency, department, commission, board, or other entity of the United States,

or

(C) an instrumentality of the United States.

Did you know that the United States is a corporation? Do you know that it is privately owned? Did you know that if you are a United States Citizen, then you are a citizen of a private corporation. This corporation is not owned by the American people. Who owns it?

"The United States Government is a foreign corporation with respect to a state" (Corpus Juris Secundum, vol. 20, sec. 1785: NY re: Merriam 36 N.E. 505 1441 S.CT. 1973, 41 L.ED.287).

Did you know that the jurisdiction of the United States government as a corporation is only the ten square miles known as the District of Columbia, the territories of the United States, military facilities, post offices, and other government buildings?

Did you know that our original government that was created by our founding fathers was unincorporated?

Why is it incorporated now?

Does this matter? Absolutely!

Does the way you capitalize your name matter? Definitely! And we will get into that shortly. If you read the Declaration of Independence, you will notice that the *u* is not capitalized in united States of America. This is different than most of us have been taught. It changed when in 1871 the new constitution was implemented for the corporate UNITED STATES OF AMERICA, a private corporation owned by the international bankers and their

Orig Not changed

allies. The small *u* in the Declaration of Independence
reflected the concept and intent of our Founding Fathers
that the original thirteen colonies were thirteen individual
nations-republics, and they and their people are sovereign.
The all capitalized UNITED STATES OF AMERICA
made the federal government supreme in its authority and
power. The UNITED STATES OF AMERICA is a private
corporation based out of the District of Columbia that
has enslaved the majority of Americans through deception
and fraud. For now let's look at why all these legal entities
use all capitals. There must be some good reason. How
did you ever get a name that is all capitalized? Did your
parents give it to you? Or did somebody else give it to you?
Why?

We all got our all caps names shortly after birth. To
illustrate this, let's looks at my own case. On September
18, 2016, at 10:25 a.m. I filed an identity theft report
with the DENTON POLICE DEPARTMENT. Here is
the narrative from this report:

> I have attached 8 documents that provide a
> narrative and proof of the incident. That said,
> Here is the info. At my birth, per my Certificate of
> Live Birth which is attached, my name is Michael
> Ray Blackwell. Next, the STATE DIRECTOR
> OF PUBLIC HEALTH AND REGISTRAR OF
> VITAL STATISTICS 'registered' my birth, via
> the Notification of Birth Registration document,

copy attached. On the 'Notification of Birth Registration' my name is Michael Ray Blackwell. This 'Notification of Birth Registration' is from the all capitalized state agency of the all capitalized STATE OF CALIFORNIA. Capitalizing and not capitalizing letters has legal significance. The STATE OF CALIFORNIA is a subsidiary of the UNITED STATES OF AMERICA, a privately owned corporation registered in the District of Columbia. This act was done without my parent's knowledge, understanding and consent. By the act, my political status from an American National to a United States citizen. This was and is an act of fraud. This act changed my political status from having God given rights protected by our Americas founding documents which are the Declaration of Independence of 1776, the Constitution of 1787 and the Bill of Rights in 1792 to having privileges granted by the United States corporate government that is privately owned. This was done without the full knowledge and understanding of my parents per my mother's two affidavits that are attached. This has been done without my consent obviously. This is fraud and identity theft.

I filed an incident report with the Denton Police Department claiming identity theft since the STATE OF CALIFORNIA, a subsidiary of the UNITED STATES

OF AMERICA, a privately owned corporation registered in the District of Columbia, upon registering my birth used all capital letters to designate my name thus changing my political status was changed from an American National to a United States citizen without my parents' informed consent. One of my supporting documents was my certificate of live birth from the county. On it my name is spelled Michael Ray Blackwell, in upper and lowercase letters. The date of the document is April 3, 1949. I was born at 7:57 a.m.

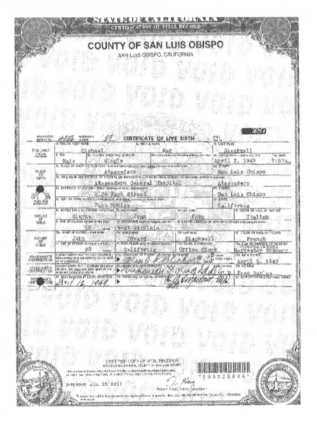

This certificate of live birth from the STATE OF CALIFORNIA, COUNTY OF SAN LUIS OBISPO, SAN LUIS OBISPO, CALIFORNIA is basically for the vital records office.

The Notification of Birth Registration issued by the STATE OF CALIFORNIA signed by the state director of public health and registrar of vital statistics. Please notice that my name is spelled Michael Ray Blackwell in upper and lowercase letters.

Then you will see my birth certificate that was issued by the Atascadero Hospital in Atascadero, California. My name is spelled in all capital letters. Why?

What is the significance of our names being spelled in upper and lowercase letters versus all capitalized letters?

It is greatly significant. It has legal and political status implications that could mean the difference between being a slave or sovereign free man or woman. Did you know that? I bet you weren't taught that in school or at home. Have you ever heard the mainstream media or an attorney or banker explain that to you?

Atascadero Hospital

Atascadero, California

BIRTH CERTIFICATE

This Certifies that MICHAEL RAY BLACKWELL

was born in Atascadero Hospital, Atascadero, California

at 7:57 A.M. on the 3rd day of APRIL A.D. 19 49

In Witness Whereof the said Hospital has caused this Certificate to be signed by its duly authorized officer and its Corporate Seal to be hereunto affixed.

MARY G. ROWE R.N. Supt

Hospital Number

Doctor

Here is what happened. As evidenced by the certificate of live birth I was born into this world on April 3, 1949 at 7:57 a.m. My name is spelled Michael Ray Blackwell, in upper and lowercase letters. I was born as a free man in California state as an American state national. This means the unincorporated California state, which is a sovereign republic, nation-state. Being born in California state with God-given rights protected by our founding documents means that I was born an American national. The all caps STATE OF CALIFORNIA is the corporate entity that is a subsidiary of the corporate UNITED STATES OF AMERICA. This indicates that my parents sold me into slavery in exchange for benefits from the corporate state, also known as the UNITED STATES OF AMERICA. At birth conferred upon me were all my God-given, unalienable rights that are protected by our founding documents of this country, which include the Declaration of Independence of 1776, the Constitution of the United States of America of 1787, the Treaty of Versailles of 1783, the Treaty of Paris 1783—which ended the revolutionary war against the British—the Bill of Rights of 1792, and all of our other founding documents.

Then when I was "registered" with the STATE DIRECTOR OF PUBLIC HEALTH AND REGISTRAR OF VITAL STATISTICS, something happened. All of a sudden, something changed. In certain documents my name became MICHAEL RAY BLACKWELL, with all capitalized letters. Why? What does it mean?

It turns out the government requires all hospitals to register newborn children with the DEPARTMENT OF VITAL STATISTICS, which is a subsidiary of the STATE OF CALIFORNIA. SAN LUIS OBISPO COUNTY is also a subsidiary of the STATE OF CALIFORNIA. The STATE OF CALIFORNIA is a subsidiary of the UNITED STATES OF AMERICA, which is a private corporation organized in WASHINGTON, DISTRICT OF COLUMBIA. This is true in every state.

Names in all capital letters signify in legal terms a corporate entity. When I was registered with the DEPARTMENT OF VITAL STATISTICS of the STATE OF CALIFORNIA, a new corporate entity was created. That corporate entity is MICHAEL RAY BLACKWELL. This entity was created by the corporate state. This corporate entity is owned by the state because the state was the creator. Why did the corporate state do this?

As Confucius (551-479 BC) said, "When words lose their meaning, people lose their liberty" (The Analects, XIII, 3).

The ramifications of this action by the corporate state are immense. We have been taught that the all caps name is us, a living, breathing, flesh-and-blood man or woman who has a body, soul, and spirit. That is not true, the all caps name is a dead corporation that is a subsidiary of the STATE OF CALIFORNIA in my case, and the state is a subsidiary of the corporation UNITED STATES OF AMERICA, as we have seen.

So, your dead corporate person, or straw man, is a corporation that is owned by the state because the state created this dead corporation without your and your parents' knowledge. The state grants privileges to corporations. Look at your driver's license issued by a state corporation. You apply for the driver's license to the state, and they grant to you the privilege to drive on their roads. If they grant you a privilege, they can rescind that privilege. This happens all the time when people are in violation of the DEPARTMENT OF MOTOR VEHICLES'S rules and the state's laws. Notice that the name on your driver's license is all caps. This is the corporation named after you. The corporation named after you is created by the STATE, and it is a dead entity. The dead entity, your all capitalized name, a corporation, is part of the kingdom of the dead.

Dead entities do not have God-given rights protected by our country's founding documents. Only living beings with a body, soul, and spirit can have God-given rights because they were created by God. Dead entities have privileges granted by the corporate government. Why does our government grant privileges? Because the UNITED STATES OF AMERICA is a corporation, it cannot grant God-given rights. Only God can grant God-given rights. The government grants privileges because it is a dead corporate entity.

When you are born, you are born a living, breathing man or woman. You are flesh and blood, with a body, soul, and spirit. You are God's creation, born through your parents who are the vessels created by God for His purpose. This woman or man is born into this world infected in a sense with sin that occurred in the fall of Adam and Eve. We are all fallen vessels in need of a savior to wash away and forgive sin so that we may become vessels for God. This is why God sent his only begotten son, Jesus the Christ—to save man. The purpose of this is to save man for God's purposes and to give dominion to God over the whole earth through God's chosen vessels. This has been happening throughout history and the Bible is the reference book.

We are born into this world to be a vessel for the Most High God. Right after birth, we are given a fake name copied after our real name. The STATE OF CALIFORNIA, through its DEPARTMENT OF VITAL

STATISTICS induced and defrauded my mother and father by informing them I had to be registered with the corporate state. They did not realize what this meant legally and how it would affect my political status.

When I was registered with the state, a dead corporate entity was created shortly after my birth, and my political status was changed from a free man with God-given rights protected by the Constitution of the United States of America and other founding documents to an economic slave to the corporate state with no God-given rights protected by the Constitution of the United States of America and other founding documents. The slave has to apply for privileges, or permission, from the corporate state, and its subsidiaries, or you could say master. What father and mother would do this to their son or daughter voluntarily? My parents were deceived and defrauded as evidenced by an affidavit my mother provided to me.

This has been done because my parents trusted the personnel at the hospital, the hospital itself, and government. This is how things work, and registration of the newborn baby is required, if you want to leave the hospital with your baby. If this was disclosed to my parents, my guess is they would not have registered me with the state.

So, basically, the state fraudulently obtained my parents signature and permission to register the baby, me.

The definition of intrinsic fraud is to not fully disclose the matter in an attempt to deceive. Therefore, the state has committed intrinsic fraud and identity theft when they in essence coerced my parents into signing away my freedom.

Hard to believe, right? Too farfetched? This is some conspiracy theory, right? How about some more evidence?

There is an interesting thing about fraud. The Latin term ab initio means "from the beginning. In legal terms regarding fraud, it means because of fraud, everything relating to the fraud is void from the beginning of the fraud. This is a very powerful tool and reality.

Did you know that any agency of the government, whether a state or the UNITED STATES OF AMERICA, is a dead corporation? So, in my case, the Department of Vital Statistics registering me with the STATE OF CALIFORNIA was an act of intrinsic fraud and identity theft. Because this was an act of fraud, you have the God-given lawful right to declare this corporate registration null and void, ab initio. The corporate entities of the corporate UNITED STATES OF AMERICA hope you never discover this fraud. If you never discover this act of fraud, you will always be a corporate citizen of the UNITED STATES OF AMERICA with only privileges and not God-given rights. According to their statutory law and rules and regulations, you are a slave and a piece of chattel over which they have complete legal control.

On the other hand, an American national has God-given unalienable rights protected by our nation's founding documents. If you are an American national, you are free. You are actually a sovereign like King George of England per the Treaties of Paris and Versailles of 1783, which ended our Revolutionary War with the British. This is what our forefathers gave to their children and their posterity. This means *you*. The form of government given to us by our forefathers was meant for living, breathing, flesh-and-blood men and women who have a body, soul, and spirit and who were a moral people. It was not for dead corporate entities.

When I say a moral people, I mean a people who are knowledgeable about the law of nature and the God of the Bible. This is how our founding documents are written. When you read them, you will realize there is a direct correlation between them and the God of the Bible. We have turned away as a nation from the morality of the Bible and have turned to the God of the dead. Today, we live and operate in the kingdom of the dead. How is that, you ask? As a corporation your all capitalized name is a dead entity. You are the chattel of a dead entity, which is your corporate government. The dead entity gives you privileges. Satan also gives privileges to his property. God gives unalienable rights. Which do you have? Which do you prefer?

The majority of the American people are dead, corporate, zombies. I hate to say that. I do know that there is a remnant of Americans that is patriotic, Christians who love this country and a revival is coming. The majority of Americans have been enslaved by their government, in cooperation with the media, schools, universities, and countless other organizations and institutions. The American people are trusting. They trusted their government. These are hard statements. You do not believe this? Keep reading and discover the truth.

So, why did the politicians decided to incorporate the UNITED STATES OF AMERICA? What was the motivation and goal of the criminal cabal that created this plan? Could their motivation be a New World Order? Could these people be satanists who hate the God of the Bible? Who are these people? Let's focus for now on the why they did this.

6

JURISDICTION

As I stated earlier, our forefathers gave to us a form of government that was "of the people, for the people, and by the people." This government was for a sovereign people according to the Treaties of Paris and Versailles in 1783. The individuals of this great nation were sovereigns. They had the same power and authority that King George of England had at that time in history.

The people assembled and created their township governments. The people assembled and created their county governments. The people assembled and created their state governments. And finally, the people, through their state assembly governments, created a federal government with nineteen specific powers. All other power resided with the states, the counties, townships, and the people. As a Christian people and nation, the people recognized that all power came from God and that God is the supreme power in the universe who created heaven and earth and all things in it. That everything is owned by God. That God has all authority. The people had the authority and power over the government. The government and its employees and agents were servants of the people. Is that what we have today in America? What happened? What went wrong?

Originally America's government was unincorporated. As I said, it was a government of the people, for the people, and by the people. In order to defraud the people it was necessary to define people. Our original government defined people as living, breathing, flesh-and-blood men and women who each has a body, soul and spirit. If you read the Declaration of Independence you will notice it says, "the united States of America." You will see that the Founding Fathers used a lower case "u" in "united." The lowercase "u" shows that we were declaring independence as thirteen individual sovereign states. We weren't a unified country yet but were called "these united States." The united States of America was an unincorporated collection of living, breathing, flesh-and-blood men and women who each has a body, soul and spirit who assembled and formed their government. After Lincoln's death the international bankers and the government they controlled, and soon owned, defrauded the nation of states by incorporating the country.

The registration of a living baby with the DEPARTMENT OF VITAL STATISTICS changed the political status of the baby from an American national who has God-given rights protected by the Constitution to a corporate citizen or the UNITED STATES OF

AMERICA who is a dead corporate entity with no God-given rights. This Supreme Court case explains the issue.

> Inasmuch, a government is an artificial person, an abstraction, and a creature of the mind only, a government can only interface with another artificial person. The imaginary, having neither actuality or substance, and it is foreclosed from creating and attaining parity with the tangible. The legal manifestation of this is that no government, as well as any law, agency, aspect, court etc. can concern itself with anything other than corporate, artificial persons, and the contract between them. (S.C.R. 1797, Penhallow v. Doane's Administrators, 3 U.S. 54; 1Led. 57; 3 Dall. 54)

Instead of being an American state national under the authority of God, who has authority over all things, including government, a UNITED STATES citizen is a piece of chattel owned by the corporate government. If you have not corrected your political status, you are operating as an inanimate corporate entity." Through fraud and identity theft, the corporate government has all authority over you. Let's look at some court cases.

> First Amendment rights are indeed fundamental, for "we the people" are the sovereigns, not those

who sit in the seats of the mighty. (BROADRICK v. OKLAHOMA, 413 U.S. 601, 1973). :

Sovereigns are equal. It is the duty of a sovereign, not to submit his rights to the decision of a co-sovereign. He is the sole arbiter of his own rights. He acknowledges no superior, but God alone. To his equals, he shows respect, but not submission." (THE SCHOONER EXCHANGE v. McFADDON, 11 U.S. 116, 1812).

Sovereignty itself is, of course, not subject to law, for it is the author and source of law; but in our system, while sovereign powers are delegated to the agencies of government, sovereignty itself remains with the people, by whom and for whom all government exists and acts. (DOWNES V. BIDWELL, 182 U.S. 244, 1901)

Please refer to appendix C for additional court cases. So, as you can see, reading the above court cases, jurisdiction is a big deal. Why is it that in some cases the courts have jurisdiction and in other cases they do not?

The corporate UNITED STATES OF AMERICA has limited jurisdiction is foreclosed or prohibited from creating and attaining parity with the tangible. Its jurisdiction is the ten square miles of WASHINGTON, DC, plus all US territories and federal facilities such as military bases, post offices, and federal facilities. Therefore, it does not have jurisdiction in the fifty sovereign nation-states, such as the Texas republic-state where I live.

So why is it that all the UNITED STATES DISTRICT COURTS throughout America claim they have jurisdiction over you. They do have jurisdiction over us, right?

How about the IRS, FBI, CIA, EPA, and all the other federal agencies? Do they have jurisdiction over us?

I used to think they had jurisdiction over each one of us. This is what I was taught, and the media and our entire society confirms this. The problem is all of the case law I have cited previously does not confirm this. In fact, it confirms the opposite.

The reality is all of the federal judiciary and federal agencies presume they have jurisdiction over you. A free man or woman has to challenge the government's jurisdiction, otherwise it is assumed they have jurisdiction because you consented to a contract with them by not challenging their jurisdiction. They know that each one of us has a birth certificate and we are chattel property of the state.

The reason they assume they have jurisdiction over each one of us is they believe each and every one of us is an inanimate corporate entity, just like them. Except, you and I are not corporate entities. We are not an artificial person, an abstraction and a creature of the mind only. And as long as you don't challenge their jurisdiction, they do have authority according to PENHALLOW v DOANE'S ADMINISTRATOR'S and US v MINKER.

What does the evidence say? Are we a corporate entity? Or are we a living, breathing, flesh-and-blood man or woman who has a body, soul, and spirit?

Here is some common evidence that declares to everyone that you are an inanimate corporate entity:

> **Driver's License.** If you look at your driver's license, you will see that your name is in all capital letters. This is the corporation that was created shortly after your birth when your parents registered you with the Department of Vital Statistics in the state in which you were born. This is commonly referred to as your straw man.

> **Bank Account.** If you look at your bank statement, your name is in all capital letters. Once again, you are declaring you are a corporate entity.

> **Social Security Card.** If you look at your social security card, your name is in all capitals. Once again, you are declaring you are a corporate entity.

> **Brokerage Account.** Check your name on your brokerage account; it will be in all capital letters.

> **Mortgage Account.** Your name on your mortgage will be in all capital letters.

Legal Documents. When you are sued by someone or the government, your name on the paperwork will be in all capitals.

Passport. Your name will be in all capital letters. You are declaring you are a citizen of the UNITED STATES OF AMERICA, the corporation under the penalty of perjury.

IRS Tax Return. Your name will be in all capital letters. When you sign your tax return you are declaring you are a citizen of the UNITED STATES OF AMERICA, the corporation, under the penalty of perjury.

Voter Registration. When you register to vote in elections, of your all capital letters county, state, and federal elections, you have declared you are a citizen of the corporate UNITED STATES OF AMERICA owned by the Rothschild's and other international bankers, who many, if not all, have set up a Satanic system of money and debt which is unlawful according to the Constitution.

Your entire life declares that you are an inanimate corporate entity. A fiction, an artificial person having neither actuality nor substance. The evidence declares that you are a corporate citizen who asks your master for privileges. These privileges are granted and identified as licenses.

If this is true about you, the courts in America today have absolute jurisdiction over you. If this is true, you are a slave of the state, and according to the state, they own you; you are their property.

You may be thinking, "it is obvious I am a live human being, so of course they do not have jurisdiction." Well, the reality is, they have plenty of evidence that you are an inanimate entity and they will proceed with the presumption that they have jurisdiction. Therefore, you have to declare the truth that you are a living, breathing man or woman repeatedly in writing because they will try to ignore you. There are solutions to the problem. We will cover them shortly.

"This is crazy," you may be saying. "It does not make sense." But it does make sense if you look at it from the corporate legal perspective of statutory law. They absolutely have control, authority, and jurisdiction of any and all corporate UNITED STATES citizens. If, you are an American state national, however, the government employees at all levels are your employees. They are here to serve you.

Today, we view them as having complete authority over us. We have to have a license to do virtually everything from marrying and driving to making a living. For example, marriage was originally between man, woman, and God. Today, if you apply for a marriage license from the corporate STATE, it grants you permission to marry. They will issue a marriage license, which legally makes them a party to the marriage. So in a civil marriage, it is the man, woman, and the government that have entered into a partnership, so to speak. The government, therefore, has a claim to any offspring from the marriage. This is why they have the legal authority to take away children from the parents if they choose to. This corporate entity, that is a creation of some human, now has legal authority to take away the children of beings who were created by God. What is the spiritual nature of this corporate entity?

Who does this make any sense to? Is this how it always has been? What is the spiritual nature of our government today? I am just asking the question. So, lets continue our studies.

7

WHAT IS AN AMERICAN NATIONAL

An American national is a live, living, flesh-and-blood man or woman who has a body, soul and spirit and lives on the land in peace and who is owed all the liberties and God-given rights as declared in our nation's founding documents. An American national lives in a nation-state in America. I live in the Republic of Texas, an independent nation-state. There are forty-nine other nation-states that make up the United States of America. These fifty nation-states are unincorporated. These fifty nation-states were created by their local county governments which are unincorporated jural assemblies. They created the United States of America, which is also unincorporated. This is a government of the people, by the people, and for the people. An American national is not a citizen of the UNITED STATES OF AMERICA, the corporation. An American national is a citizen of the united States of America, unincorporated.

An American national is subject to the American common law and to the common law of the individual nation-state in which they live. An American national is not subject to statutory law unless he consents. An American national is also subject to God's law as described in the Bible. An American national hopefully has God's law inscribed in his heart because he has studied the Word of God. An American national is subject to God's law.

An American national is owed the law of the land. Most people believe that any statute passed by Congress and signed by the president is the law of the land. This is simply not true. The US Constitution is the supreme law of the land, and any statute to be valid must be in agreement. Therefore, it is impossible for both the Constitution and a law violating it to be valid.

> The general rule is that an unconstitutional statute, though having the form and name of law, is in reality no law, but is wholly void, and ineffective for any purpose; since unconstitutionality dates from the time of its enactment, and not merely from the date of the decision so branding it. An unconstitutional law, in legal contemplation, is as inoperative as if it had never been passed. Such a statute leaves the question that it purports to settle just as it would be had the statute not been enacted.

Such an unconstitutional law is void, the general principles follow that it imposes no duties, confers no rights, creates no office, bestows no power or authority on anyone, affords no protection, and justifies no acts performed under it.

A void act cannot be legally consistent with a valid one. An unconstitutional law cannot operate to supersede any existing valid law. Indeed, insofar as a statue runs counter to the fundamental law of the land, it is superseded thereby.

No one is bound to obey an unconstitutional law and no courts are bound to enforce it. (Sixteenth *American Jurisprudence*, second edition, sec. 177)

And in Article Six, Section Two of the Constitution of the United States we read:

This Constitution, and the Laws of the United States which shall be made in Pursuance thereof; and all Treaties made, or which shall be made, under the Authority of the United States, shall be the SUPREME LAW OF THE LAND; and the JUDGES IN EVERY STATE SHALL BE BOUND THEREBY, any thing in the Constitution or Laws of any State to the Contrary notwithstanding.

In appendix E is an affidavit I have used to explain my political status. It explains the difference between a corporate UNITED STATES OF AMERICAN citizen and an American national. It also explains the Fourteenth Amendment pretty well.

No "citizen of the United States" has a domicile except in D.C. where a citizen of the United States is a qualified Elector.

Once again, the corporate UNITED STATES OF AMERICA is located in the District of Columbia. Yet, you claim that you are a citizen of the UNITED STATES OF AMERICA. Do you have a domicile in the District of Columbia?

If you are a citizen of the UNITED STATES OF AMERICA, the corporation, you are a citizen of a dead corporate entity. According to evidence we discussed earlier, you probably are a citizen of a dead corporation that is privately owned. Who owns this private corporation. Are they godly men or are they satanists? What is the fruit or character today of this corporate government?

Did you know, only "citizens of the several States" as proclaimed in the Declaration of Independence have a Creator. "We hold these truths to be self-evidence, that all men are created equal. That they are endowed by their Creator with certain unalienable Rights, that among these are Life, Liberty and the pursuit of Happiness."

Man's statutory creations *do* not have this, which also includes corporations, limited liability partnerships, and the like, and therein is the logic that "citizens of the "United States" have no Creator!

So, do you have a Creator? Why are you a citizen of the corporate UNITED STATES OF AMERICA, a dead entity, then? What is the spiritual nature of a dead entity?

Did you know that we do have a lawful government of the people, by the people, and for the people? Did you know that it is composed of men and women who do have a Creator, and it operates according to our founding documents, the Declaration of Independence of 1776, the Treaties of Paris and Versailles of 1783, the Constitution of 1787 and the Bill of Rights of 1792?

Let's continue our studies.

8

WHERE DOES AUTHORITY COME FROM?

Our forefather's rebelled against the greatest power in the world at the time, the English Empire. Where did our forefather's think they had the authority to do this? Here are their words in the Declaration of Independence:

> The unanimous Declaration of the thirteen united States of America, When in the Course of human events, it becomes necessary for one people to dissolve the political bands which have connected them with another, and to assume among the powers of the earth, the separate and equal station to which the Laws of Nature and of Nature's God entitle them, a decent respect to the opinions of mankind requires that they should declare the causes which impel them to the separation.

Our forefather's derived their authority from "the Laws of Nature and of Nature's God." This is the God of the Bible, the Great I AM.

The Holy Bible says:

> Then God said, "Let Us make man in Our image, according to Our likeness; let them have dominion over the fish of the sea and over the birds of the air, and over the cattle, over all the earth and over every creeping thing that creeps upon the earth." So God created man in His own image; in the image of God He created him; male and female He created them. Then God Blessed them; and God said to them, "Be fruitful and multiply; fill the earth and subdue it; have dominion over the fish of the sea and over the birds of the air, and over every living thing that moves on the earth." (Genesis 1:26-28)

As we can see, *all authority* comes from *God*.

It is crystal clear that the God of the Bible delegated his authority, as the Creator of heaven and earth, and everything in it, to man. He is the One and only God. The true, sovereign God delegated his authority to a living, breathing, flesh-and-blood man, Adam. Adam sinned. Later, God delegated His Authority to Jesus, the Christ. Jesus Christ delegated this authority to the church.

Our forefather's risked and based the lives of themselves, their families, their friends and their revolution, for a future nation and government on God's word.

The rest is our great American history. They prevailed through faith, persistence, and trusting in God. (See appendix D for more Scripture of where our authority comes from.)

I believe the Holy Bible to be the absolute Word of the living God. That the one and only living God, delegated his authority on earth to man through Adam, the first man, and then to Jesus Christ, the second man, the new man who is a proto type of the new creation. The new man has God's Spirit added to him. So, when a sinner calls upon God to save him through his son, Jesus Christ, God does save this sinner by adding his element, or Spirit to him. God's Spirit becomes mingled with the human spirit and transformation begins. This is what Jesus meant in telling Nicodemus he "must be born again." Before Jesus Christ left this earth, he delegated his authority to the church.

As this relates to human events on earth, our forefather's obtained their authority to rebel against England, the greatest power on earth at the time, and create a new country and government based upon God's Word and authority and instituted this concept in our government. This is evidenced in our founding documents and many writings of our founders.

9

WHAT IS THE MOTIVATION
OF THE FRAUD?

The motivation is pretty simple, money and power. Or could it be more than just money and power? I think it is. It is spiritual power and authority on who controls earth and the people on earth. Let's review what happened. When the corporate state and its subsidiaries, agencies, and departments register each newborn baby with the DEPARTMENT OF VITAL STATISTICS for each state it changes the baby's political status without the baby, the mother's or the father's understanding. The baby's political status was changed from a baby created by God through the parents with God-given unalienable rights—a free sovereign person—to the political status of a slave, with privileges given to the baby by the master, which is the corporate government of the UNITED STATES OF AMERICA. These privileges may be canceled by the corporate government and their agents if the slave does not obey the orders, rules, laws, regulations of the corporate state.

This action of registering the baby with the DEPARTMENT OF VITAL STATISTICS is an act of intrinsic fraud and identity theft. It is an act of conspiracy to obtain absolute jurisdiction over the free, sovereign being. These acts are crimes with the intent to steal, defraud, and enslave the free sovereign person. Looking at this through spiritual eyes, who is the author of all lies? Well, Satan is. Is intrinsic fraud and identity theft in God's nature? No. Is it in Satan's nature? Yes.

It simply gets back to this case law:

> Inasmuch as every government is an artificial person, an abstraction, and a creature of the mind only, a government can interface only with other artificial persons. The imaginary, having neither actuality nor substance, is foreclosed from creating and attaining parity with the tangible. The legal manifestation of this is that no government, as well as any law, agency, aspect, court, etc. can concern itself with anything other than corporate, artificial persons and the contracts between them. (US v Minker, 350 US 179 at 187, 1956)

So the corporate government created a dead corporation named after you at birth so that they could fraudulently claim you and convince you that the dead corporation was actually you, the living, breathing, flesh-and-blood man (or woman) who has a body, soul, and spirit created by God. You, the living, breathing, flesh-and-blood man (or woman) who has a body, soul, and spirit is free and under only American common law according to our founding documents. You, the living man (or woman), is sovereign and the employees of the corporate government work for you. If they do not, they are liable. The dead corporate government created a dead entity that has your name in all capital letters, so they could gain jurisdiction over you. Once the dead corporate government gained this jurisdiction over you by fraud and identity theft, they are in position to steal your money, your property and your life. They do this by lies and deception. The reality is 99.99 percent of Americans have no idea this happened to them. They believe the all capitalized name on their driver's license, passport, and other legal documents is them. What a great deception and they are easy prey for the powers that be.

So, let me ask you, what is the spiritual nature of someone, or some entity that operates on deceit and fraud? It certainly is not the nature of the God of the Bible. Who is the father of all lies? Satan is, according to Scripture:

> You are of your father the devil, and the desires of
> your father you want to do. He was a murderer
> from the beginning, and does not stand in the
> truth, because there is no truth in him. When he

speaks a lie, he speaks from his own resources; for he is a liar and the father of it. (John 8:44)

And no wonder, for Satan himself transfigures himself into an angel of light. (2 Corinthians 11:14)

But I fear lest somehow, as the serpent deceived Eve by his craftiness, your minds would be corrupted from the simplicity that is in Christ. (2 Corinthians 11:3)

Put on the whole armor of God, that you may be able to stand against the wiles of the devil. For we do not wrestle against flesh and blood, but against principalities, against powers, against the rulers of darkness of this age, against the spiritual hosts of wickedness in the heavenly places. (Ephesians 6:11-12)

So the great dragon was cast out, that serpent of old, called the Devil and Satan, who deceives the whole world; he was cast to the earth, and his angels were cast down with him. (Revelation 12:9) And cast him into the bottomless pit, and shut him up, and set a seal on him, so that he should deceive the nations no more till the thousand years were finished; But after these things he must be released for a little while. (Revelation 20:3)

There are many more Scriptures I could add, but you have the general idea. We live in an age of great deception, Satan, the Devil is the father of all lies and the chief deceiver. Is it so farfetched to think that there is a spiritual nature to the Birth Certificate Fraud and Identity Theft Fraud I have disclosed? Please look at the information I have presented carefully and consider the facts.

10

A QUOTE OF
PRESIDENT JOHN F. KENNEDY

O n April 27, 1961, President John F. Kennedy in an address to newspaper publishers stated the following:

> The very word "secrecy" is repugnant in a free and open society, and we are as a people, inherently and historically, opposed to secret societies, secret oaths, and secret proceedings… For we are opposed around the world by a monolithic and ruthless conspiracy that relies primarily on covert means for expanding its sphere of influence. It depends on infiltration instead of invasion, on subversion instead of elections, on intimidation instead of free choice. It is a system which has conscripted vast human and material resources into the building of a tightly knit, highly efficient machine that combines military, diplomatic, intelligence,

economic, scientific, and political operations. Its preparations are concealed, not published, its mistakes are buried, not headlined, its dissenters are silenced, not praised, no expenditure is questioned, no secret is revealed... I am asking your help in the tremendous task of informing and alerting the American people... The high office of President has been used to foment a plot to destroy the American's freedom, and before I leave office I must inform the citizen of his plight."

President John F. Kennedy was assassinated on November 22, 1963.

Did President John F. Kennedy understand the spiritual, criminal conspiracy of the international bankers, globalists, New World Order, satanist, secret societies? Yes he did. This is why he signed an executive order several weeks before his death instructing the US Treasury to prepare to issue silver-backed money. This was a direct threat to the Federal Reserve System , which is neither federal or a reserve. This executive order would have eliminated the Federal Reserve operating in America, which is owned by the international bankers and satanists. The central banking system is one part of the conspiracy to enslave the American people. President John F. Kennedy was in the process of exposing the criminal cabal and freeing the American people from monetary enslavement. President Kennedy was assassinated several weeks later.

Another interesting point is that all wars are banker wars. Wars are probably the biggest money makers for the international banking criminal cabal. The international bankers want war for profit. Satan wants war, for he comes to kill, steal, and destroy.

I stated earlier, that my brother Rock was a Special Forces advisor in the Republic of South Vietnam from 1963-1965. About a month prior to the Kennedy assassination, American advisors were given the order to pack up their gear; they all were coming home. They were told that Kennedy was not going to allow America to be engaged in a major land war in Southeast Asia. Rock and his teammates were actually packing up their gear and equipment to come home. Shortly thereafter, Kennedy was assassinated. Shortly after that, President Johnson announced a major buildup of American forces in the Republic of South Vietnam.

Remember, international bankers and satanists love war.

11

TREASON

There is a criminal conspiracy against the people of America. Specifically the powers of the world cannot stand America's original government that was created by our forefathers. Our nation was founded as a Christian nation that put its trust in the God of the Bible, the Creator of the universe who is identified in the Holy Bible. Our forefathers created a nation for a Christian people who trusted their God. Our founding documents attest to this fact.

According to the Treaty of Paris and the Treaty of Versailles the American victors and their land were declared sovereign. There were also other Americans who were British loyalists in America, and they were allowed to retain their loyalty to England per the treaties.

The American patriots were governed by American common law, which is the law of the land. The people in America who chose to remain loyal to England were governed by admiralty law, which is maritime law or the law of the sea.

Throughout history there has been a struggle for power in America. That struggle is basically between two forces. The first is the people that believe in our form of government as founded by our forefathers and wish to retain their freedom and political status. The other group is people who wish to change our form of government so that it operates according to man's law and wisdom, not God's law. There are many other sub-groups in each group.

In the group that wants to change our form of government you have the communists, fascists, socialists, satanists, big government, sharia law advocates, business interests, financiers, politicians, and more. The list is virtually endless.

Never in the history of the world, as a nation been founded upon God's laws and principals, except the nation of Israel in the Old Testament times. Never in the history of the world has a nation been founded that declared the people were the sovereigns, not the state. Never in the world has a people trusted and honored the God of the Bible in such a way, except the nation of Israel in the Bible.

Today, you have the international globalists, bankers, business interests, satanist's, and others who are moving all of us on this planet to a New World Order. To accomplish this, they have to destroy America's government as founded and to destroy America economically and militarily. From this perspective, the bad trade deals our leaders have made since John F. Kennedy's assignation begin to make sense. You begin to see how the powers that be have worn down our military through endless wars while cutting defense spending. You begin to understand all the regulations that have limited America's productivity. You begin to see why our preachers, pastors and churches have diluted the Word of God.

I am reminded of the following quote from Ronald Reagan:

> Freedom is never more than one generation away
> from extinction. We didn't pass it to our children in
> the bloodstream. It must be fought for, protected,
> and handed on for them to do the same, or one day
> we will spend our sunset years telling our children
> and our children's children what it was once like in
> the United States where men were free.

Since the founding of America, these political battles and sometimes wars have been occurring. Then, in 1860 things changed in a big way.

In 1860, Abraham Lincoln was elected president. There were fierce debates and threats prior to Lincoln's election. In the 1850s there were debates and civil unrest concerning the morality of slavery and the Southern states' need for cheap labor and to maintain their traditions.

There were many in the North that wanted the slaves freed. The truth is, there were many in the South who were freeing their slaves on their own. The industrial North was taking actions that suppressed the price of cotton, which was the major export of the Southern states. The Northern states controlled the cotton market. Since cotton was the major export of the Southern states, tempers were hot prior to the 1860 election. There was a great divide in the nation of opposing views, and it seemed that all peaceful discussion and negotiation between the two sides were going nowhere.

It reminds me of today, where our country has been divided by our political leaders and parties. You can see the individual groups dividing the people in their specific interests. It seems like we Americans are heading for real trouble. On the positive side, I do believe the American people are waking up to the fact that we are all Americans and do not and need not to be divided. I also believe that there is a spiritual awakening occurring, and Americans are turning to the true and living Word of God. Revival is on the way.

All the things mentioned above were not the main reason for the so-called Civil War. The reality is that Abraham Lincoln was a lawyer and a member of the BAR (British Accredited Registry). All American lawyers who are members of the American BAR take an oath of loyalty to the American BAR, which places their loyalty to the British Accredited Registry above any other oaths they take. This is a problem. This is basically a title of nobility as they are loyal to the British Crown.

Article 1, section 9 of the US Constitution specifies: "No Title of Nobility shall be granted by the United States: And no Person holding any Office of Profit or Trust under them, shall, without the Consent of the Congress, accept of any present, Emolument, Office, or Title of any kind whatever, from any King, Prince or foreign State."

The original Thirteenth Amendment prohibited lawyers, attorneys who were members of the BAR from being in our government. So, when Lincoln was running for president in 1860, the objection of the Southern states was primarily that he was ineligible to be president of the United States of America, unincorporated per the Constitution of 1787 and the Thirteenth Amendment.

When Abraham Lincoln won the election in 1860 the Southern states viewed Lincoln as ineligible and therefore the election as being void. In the first of the year in 1861 the Southern states refused to send their congressional delegations to Congress. With the Southern states not sending their delegations to Congress in 1861, Congress did not have a quorum (minimum number of members to convene). Congress could not open for business. It was the Southern states strategy to peacefully object to an ineligible president based upon the law of the land, the Constitution and the Bill of Rights.

The Northern states were incensed. They proceeded to make Abraham Lincoln president anyway. Once Abraham

Lincoln became president (unlawfully), Lincoln ordered a recruitment of troops to be trained and dispatched to restore order in the Southern states. The Southern states, upon hearing that Lincoln was raising an army to restore federal order, began to respond as individual states to defend their homes and land from the Northern invaders.

The Southern states had acted lawfully and peacefully to the election of an ineligible candidate of the office of the president of the United States of America, unincorporated. The Northern states acted unlawfully. To make matters worse, as Fort Sumter, South Carolina, was fired upon by the South and the Northern forces prepared to invade the Southern states, the North never declared war. The North could not declare war since Congress was not in session for lack of a quorum. As of the writing of this book, Congress has never been lawfully reassembled.

History goes to the victor though, so these are things you won't be taught in school.

Did you know that there has never been a peace treaty ending the Civil War? General Robert E. Lee did surrender the Army of Northern Virginia to General Ulysses Grant of the Union Army in April 1865. General Robert E. Lee did not, however, have the authority to surrender the Confederate States of America. Since Congress never declared an act of war against the Confederate States of America, due to never having a quorum, and there was never a peace treaty, there was never an official war. It was definitely a war, but legally it never happened.

You may call it an act of martial law, but it was not an official war.

In 1863 Lincoln issued General Order No. 100. This order is known as Instructions for the Government of the Armies of the United States in the Field. It is also known as the Lieber Code dated April 24, 1863. This general order has never been rescinded in 156 years. Why? Today, the UNITED STATES OF AMERICA, incorporated, operates under this order. Why?

Why do we have military courts using admiralty law (law of the sea) when Americans are guaranteed American common law in their courts? Could this be why the courts ignore the Constitution and the Bill of Rights to the best of their ability? These military courts were used after the ending of hostilities between the North and the South. They were part of the rebuilding of the South. They dispensed military justice as the judges saw fit. The judges were recruited from Northern sympathizers in the South and from Northern judges. These courts were used to rape and pillage the property of the South and their people. They were an important part of the Northern carpetbaggers' tools in taking advantage of the losers of the North-South conflict.

These military courts or tribunals are still in operation today throughout the UNITED STATES OF AMERICA, incorporated. Why? These courts are still operating as tools for the carpetbaggers in taking advantage of the citizens of the UNITED STATES, incorporated, and others who are assumed to be citizens of the UNITED STATES, incorporated.

These military courts or tribunals operate according to admiralty law or statutory law and attorneys who are licensed by the BAR (British Accredited Registry) are licensed to practice law in these courts. These courts are still subject to this Supreme Court ruling among many others.

> Inasmuch as every government is an artificial person, an abstraction, and a creature of the mind only, a government can interface only with other artificial persons. The imaginary, having neither actuality nor substance, is foreclosed from creating and attaining parity with the tangible. The legal manifestation of this is that no government, as well as any law, agency, aspect, court, etc. can concern itself with anything other than corporate, artificial persons and the contracts between them. (US v Minker, 350 US 179 at 187, 1956)

In 1868, the unlawful Congress (since Congress has never had a quorum since the Southern states refused to send their congressional delegations to Congress in 1861) wrote itself a new corporate constitution called "the Constitution of the United States of America." This constitution is a fraud in several areas. Notice the phrase "of the United States of America." Our original

Constitution used the phrase "for the United States of America." The constitution of 1868 has some deceptive lawyer tricks in it regarding words and capitalizations. This new constitution is void because it's a fraud. The corporate Congress of 1868 lacked lawful authority to create a new constitution and replace the original Constitution. The original states (unincorporated) of the union which never have been reassembled since 1861 for Congress to reconvene is still the law of the land. As I write this, the original unincorporated states are assembling with the intent of reconvening the lawful Congress which has been in abeyance since 1861.

In 1871, the corporate Congress created its own jurisdiction by creating a separate government for the District of Columbia. Over the years, all states have been incorporated, changing the jurisdiction from the land (American common law) to the law of the sea (admiralty law). That means today we effectively do not have the government that was given to us by our forefathers. It has been stolen from us by the powers that be, which include international financiers, banksters, corporate politicians, crooks, thieves, fraudsters, satanists, globalists and others.

Today, most Americans believe they live in a Democracy and have to obey statutory law, have to obtain a license to make a living, and have to obey all the other laws, rules, and regulations. The truth is, they do, because they are corporate citizens of the state and have no clue of their true heritage. Most Americans have turned away from the Bible, which was so important to our forefathers. I am sure this didn't just happen. It was by design and was implemented slowly over many years by powerful forces— powerful bankers and powerful spiritual forces. There are many secret and semi-secret societies and groups who desired this outcome for America. What do you think? Was this by design or by happenstance?

All members of the BAR (British Accredited Registry) practice law in these military courts. The members of the BAR are aware or should be aware that according to are founding documents we are entitled to American common law courts where BAR members are not allowed. For American BAR members, they are committing numerous crimes against the united States of America (unincorporated) and the American people.

All BAR (British Accredited Registry) members are foreign agents of the Crown. It is a private corporation domiciled in the city of London. The city of London is a walled city that is approximately two square miles. It is a separate jurisdiction from the rest of England. It is foreign to the rest of England just like the District of Columbia is foreign to each separate Republic/states in America. This Crown is owned and controlled by the Vatican.

This is why are forefathers approved the original Thirteenth Amendment prohibiting titles of nobility in government. The original Thirteenth Amendment has somehow disappeared. Why is that? Who had the authority to remove it? Congress did not disclose this to the American people, and besides, we have had an unlawful Congress since 1861. This amendment was apparently burned when the British attacked the capital and burned parts of it to the ground in the War of 1812. Thereafter, somehow it has been removed from our history. No one had authority to remove the original Thirteenth Amendment except the people who were not dead corporations but were living, breathing, flesh-and-blood men and women with a body, soul, and spirit.

Only the lawful government could replace or repeal an amendment, but the lawful government has been dormant since 1861. Since today most politicians are BAR (British Accredited Registry) members who are foreign agents of the Crown as defined in law and their own documents and oaths, it is obvious why they wouldn't want an amendment like that in place.

It is not just American BAR (British Accredited Registry) who are committing these crimes, it is every government employee who is not abiding by the original Constitution of 1787, the Declaration of Independence of 1776 and the Bill of Rights of 1792.

So, what crimes are this satanic criminal cabal committing against the American people? (See appendix F for a complete list.)

There are many good men and women who work for the corporate federal, state, county governments and their agencies. Most of them have been deceived also. No wonder the powers that be want control of education and the media.

What is interesting is that admiralty law and martial law applies to citizens of the UNITED STATES, incorporated, which includes all employees of the corporate federal, state, county, and city governments. All these laws that are statutes, rules, and regulations apply to them. These corporate citizens have a responsibility to obey those laws. If they do not, they are liable to the corporate government and the people. If the corporate government employees in dealing with an American state national do not obey and adhere to their laws, rules, and regulations, then they become personally liable to the American state national. The American state national may seek recourse against corporate government employees by going after their corporate bond or seeking damages from the individual corporate government employee.

This actually puts the American state national in a very strong lawful position. The problem is going to be finding justice in their courts. This is why American state nationals are reassembling their county jural assemblies and are in the process of setting up common law courts. The American people are waking up to the fraud and criminality of the criminal cabal.

So in summary, we the American people, who are lawfully known as American nationals, who are living, breathing flesh-and-blood men and women who live on the land in America with God-given inalienable rights protected by our founding documents have not had a lawful unincorporated government since early 1861 when our Congress did not have a quorum. Since the US Constitution of 1787 is the supreme law of the land, any form, image, or false government is and has been unlawful. The incorporated UNITED STATES OF AMERICA has been operating fraudulently since the time it was created in 1871.

The incorporated UNITED STATES OF AMERICA government gained power through fraud, lies, deceit, and force. If you are a United States citizen and your name is written in all capital letters, this is your government. If you choose to operate under an all capitalized name, you have chosen to be property and a slave of a private corporation that gives you privileges and that you give homage to in the form of taxes, fees, and obedience. Is there spiritual significance to this? Absolutely! When you choose to honor a liar, a deceiver, a fraud, a murderer, a killer of babies, a law giver that enslaves and creates bondage, who do you think you are worshipping?

You can be an unincorporated united States citizen by choice by simply being an American national. This man or woman lives and operates under God's law. He or she is regulated by the God of the Bible, who writes his laws on their hearts. This God of the Bible is a loving God, who brings freedom. His yoke is light and easy while the yoke of the liar and deceiver is bondage and death. America's founding documents are based upon God's law.

I am an American national, who is a citizen of the unincorporated united States of America by birth. This is my heritage.

As I mentioned this fraud started in the spring of 1861 when there was not a quorum in Congress. Lincoln and his allies operated in a fraudulent and emergency manner because of a lack of a quorum in Congress and Lincoln enacted the Libier Code, which was Executive Order No. 100 in 1863. This is still in effect. It is essentially martial law.

The powers that be in 1861 acted unlawfully and with malice against the Southern states. The Northern states invaded the Southern states to enforce their will upon them. This was unlawful and unconstitutional. The Southern states fought until they were defeated militarily, economically, and physically.

Reconstruction began and there was a new sheriff in town. It was the UNITED STATES OF AMERICA, incorporated, based out of WASHINGTON, DC. It is time to define two words so that we are all crystal clear. Below are the definitions for *sedition* and *treason*, according to the LawDictionary.org, featuring *Black's Law Dictionary* Free Online Legal Dictionary, 2nd Ed.

What Is Sedition?

An insurrectionary movement tending towards treason, but wanting an overt act; attempts made by meetings or speeches, or by publications, to disturb the tranquility of the state. The distinction between "sedition" and "treason" consists in this: that though the ultimate object of sedition is a violation of the public peace, or at least such a course of measures as evidently engenders it. Yet it does not aim at direct and open violence against the laws or the subversion of the constitution. Alis. Crim. Law, 5S0. In Scottish laws, the raising commotions or disturbances in the state. It is a revolt against legitimate authority. Ersk. Inst 4, 4, 14. In English law, Sedition is the offense of publishing, verbally or otherwise, any words or document with the intention of exciting disaffection, hatred, or contempt against the sovereign, or the government and constitution of the kingdom, or either house of parliament, or the administration of justice. or of exciting his majesty's subjects to attempt, otherwise than by lawful means, the alteration of any matter in church or state, or of exciting feelings of ill will and hostility between different classes of his majesty's subjects. Sweet. And see State v. Shepherd, 177 Mo. 205. 76 S. W. 79, 99 Am. St. Rep. 624.1

What Is Treason

The offense of attempting to overthrow the government of the state to which the offender owes allegiance; or of betraying the state into the hands of a foreign power. Webster. In England, treason is an offense particularly directed against the person of the sovereign, and consists (1) incompassing or imagining the death of the king or queen, or their eldest son and heir; (2) in violating the king's companion, or the king's eldest daughter unmarried, or the wife of the king's eldest son and heir; (3) in levying_war against the king in his realm; (4) in adhering to the king's enemies in his realm, giving to them aid and comfort in the realm or elsewhere, and (5) slaying the chancellor, treasurer, or the king's justices of the oue bench or the other, justices in eyre, or justices of assize, and all other justices assigned to hear and determine, being in their places doing their offices. 4 Steph. Comm. 1S5-103; 4 Bl. Comm. 76-84. "Treason against the United States shall consist only in levying war against them, or in adhering to their enemies, giving them aid and comfort." U. S. Const, art 3,2.

Now that we've defined our terms, let's take a look at what sort of sedition and treason was committed against the unsuspecting American nationals.

In 1783 when the Treaties of Paris and Versailles were signed, the united States of America was finally created and acknowledged by the world powers. This did not mean that there were not foreign and financial interests that wanted to influence, control, or actually take over this new nation called the united States of America. In fact, it is somewhat miraculous that our nation survived the first thirty years.

War finally broke out with England once again in 1812. In the above referenced peace treaties England was given control of the seas in exchange for the British protecting our young country's merchant ships. The British Navy protected American ships, but it also hijacked many American merchant seamen into the British Royal Navy. During the War of 1812 British forces actually invaded our nation's capital and burned a good part of it down.

There was a struggle for the new nation. It included many international financiers, including the Rothchilds. The financiers wanted financial control of the nation via a central bank. The nations first central bank was the Bank of North America. It was created in 1782 and lasted to 1785. Next was the First Bank of the United States which operated from 1791 to 1811. During the War of 1812 there was not a central bank in operation.

The international bankers were trying to set up their central bank system but could not get it quite right due to major resistance by the public and some politicians. Then in 1816 they had success in setting up the Second Bank of the United States, which operated until 1836. President Andrew Jackson hated central banks, stating that it was nothing but an engine of corruption. He did not renew the banks charter when it came up for renewal.

Today, President Trump has a picture of Pres
Jackson in his office. Is President Trump sign
intention is to end the Federal Reserve Bank?

It is against conventional wisdom, but the actions
of Abe Lincoln and the Northern states were against the
Constitution and the rule of law. They were not lawful and
therefore treasonous. The international bankers decided
to back the Northern states. This was the opportunity
for Rothchild and his friends to step in with funds in
exchange for opportunity. The National Banking Act of
1863 created a national banking system. In exchange,
the North received loans to finance their war efforts. The
National Banking Act operated until 1913.

In the meantime, the unlawful, unassembled
"congress" of 1868 wrote themselves a new corporate
constitution exactly like our original Constitution except
with a few wording and capitalization changes in an attempt
to deceive the American people. They were successful in
slipping it past the people, since the majority of Americans
were busy trying to recover from the ruin of the so-called
civil war. This new corporate constitution is nothing more
than corporate minutes of a private corporation. It has
nothing to do with our lawful government . . . except they
are acting as our lawful government.

In 1871 the corporate government began to set itself
up by creating a separate government for the District of
Columbia. This is the origin of the government today
in the UNITED STATES OF AMERICA. This is the

corporate government that most Americans know and love today. This is the government of which most American are citizens. If your name is in all capital letters, and you claim you are a UNITED STATES CITIZEN, then you are a citizen of a private corporation owned by the Rothchilds and the international financiers who are their friends and partners in this endeavor. These acts by the unlawful congress were continued acts of fraud and treason against the American people and the original US Constitution.

On the evening of December 23, 1913, most of the members of the unlawful congress had left for the Christmas holidays. The remaining members, who barely had a quorum, passed the Federal Reserve Act. This gave the Rothchilds and the international bankers complete control of our money system. This gave the international bankers a legal right to create paper money out of the thin air from nothing. They then lend this created-from-nothing paper note to our government and to the people and charge us compound interest. The Federal Reserve banks now use our own credit and make us liable for compelled performance for the privilege. The Federal Reserve does not use their wealth or property to back this debt note, which we are required by law to use as legal tender.

For twenty years, the United States paid the interest in gold to the international bankers. In 1933, there was no more gold in the treasury, and the United States declared bankruptcy. Was this a plan by the Rothchilds and their international bankers to fraudulently steal the gold out of the US Treasury in exchange for nothing? It sure looks like it. The plot continues. In bankruptcy, the United States went into receivership and reorganized for the benefit of its creditors and new owners. Who were the creditors and the new owners? Is this our lawful government? No, it is not. It is simply a private corporation who stole our gold.

In 1932, Franklin D. Roosevelt was elected president. His background was as an investment banker from New York. When he took office, he immediately did several things. He promoted and passed the New Deal, which was a huge move towards socialism and a control economy away from free markets. He also made it illegal for Americans to own gold. These two actions were and are in violation of our original Constitution. Of course, he was not acting under the lawful authority from the original Constitution because our lawful Congress had not reassembled since 1861. He was acting for and on behalf of the corporate UNITED STATES OF AMERICA.

A third act of Roosevelt, which is horrible, was he required that everyone have a Social Security number. In the language of the original bill, it states that anyone who has a Social Security number is incapable of handling their own affairs, and therefore, they have become a ward of the state. If you are a ward of the state, do you have control of your life? Do you have freedom and liberty? Prior to this, all family births were kept in the family Bible. Now the state keeps all these records via mandatory birth certificates. Like the issue of the fraudulent birth certificates, which we discussed earlier, the Social Security number also makes you a ward of the corporate state.

If you have a bank account, your name is in all capitals. This identifies you as a corporate UNITED STATES citizen. If you have a Social Security number, this identifies you as a corporate UNITED STATES citizen. If you file a UNITED STATES tax return, you swear under the penalty of perjury that you are a corporate UNITED STATES citizen. Have you tried to get a loan from a bank without these three items? It will not happen.

Have you tried to work without a license? It is very difficult. Everything today in our economic system is to bring a benefit to the corporate UNITED STATES citizen. Why is that?

What if I choose a political status of an American state national? I am simply stating that I am a living, breathing, flesh-and-blood man or woman who has a body, soul, and spirit who was created by God with unalienable God-given rights protected by our original US Constitution. I am also stating when I choose a political status of an American state national, I am a united States citizen by birthright who lives and operates on the land in peace per our original Constitution. This is a problem for the powers that be. Why is that?

The reason is simple. It is all about the corporate state's pursuit of power, jurisdiction, and authority over you, the living, breathing, flesh-and-blood man or woman who has a body, soul, and spirit. They only have jurisdiction over the dead corporate entity that they created fraudulently. Once again, I ask you, is there a spiritual component to this?

Here is their plan and goal. From the beginning, the powers that be, the Rothchilds and their international banker friends and associates, formed a criminal cabal to plunder, conquer, and enslave the people of the united States of America who won their independence from England and created a form of government never before seen on planet earth, and never since duplicated.

It was audacious of these American colonists to fight—and defeat—the greatest power on earth at the time. These American revolutionaries even had the audacity to form a government based upon the law of the God of the Bible and common law. They made the common man or woman in America on equal footing with the same God-given rights as the king of England! This is proven by the many court cases I have cited previously. How outrageous!

As discussed previously, powerful financial and political interests wanted to conquer America either outright militarily or by deception. These acts that we have discussed are all acts of fraud and treason against our constitutional government that our forefathers gave us. The plan, the scheme, or whatever you want to call it, is so outrageous, no one would believe it. Yet, it happened. It is our history.

You can really see this when you study America's true history from President John F. Kennedy's assassination to our current affairs. If Hillary Clinton would have won the 2016 election, the crime would have been completed as she would have moved us into the socialist New World Order. But by the tender mercies and grace of the almighty God of the Bible she did not win. The battle still rages. This battle has a spiritual nature to it. Look at the parties in the battle and how they operate to discern the spiritual nature of the battle. There are powerful spiritual forces that have directed this plan of the destruction of the United States since at least 1860. It is a battle of good versus evil. It is a part of the battle between the God of the Bible and Satan on who will control planet earth and mankind.

Are you going to be oblivious to the truth? Are you not wanting to choose a side? Are you going to be intimated into inaction and not care? Are you going to believe the lie or the truth? There is not a middle ground. The way this works spiritually is, you are going to choose either the God of the Bible or Satan. Once again, there is no middle ground. So, my question to you is, who do you choose to serve and align with? May you choose wisely.

12

THE SOLUTION

An acquaintance of mine asked me, What do I do to be free? Should I call my state? Is there a list of questions I should ask when I call? The problem is if you call your STATE, the person who answers the phone is an employee of the STATE, in my case, the STATE OF TEXAS, a corporate entity that is a subsidiary of the UNITED STATES OF AMERICA, INC. The individuals who answer the phone may be good people, but in all probability, they will have no idea what you are talking about. They are just like you and me. We were all born and raised into this system. It is very similar to the movie the *Matrix*. If you have questions that you wish to ask them, go ahead and ask, but good luck getting answers.

Another question I was asked is Do we need to contact an American state national attorney? There is no such thing. An attorney is not allowed to practice American common law. They practice a foreign law that has been patented by the Vatican. Any attorney, even if they are your friend or family member, cannot help you. They have sworn an allegiance to the crown and the BAR. Whether they realize it or not, they are part of the global corporate state as the world has moved into the New World Order. They need to wake up and see where they are headed spiritually. There are counselors-at-law. These are people who are familiar with the law but are not licensed BAR members.

Another question I was asked is, "Are there steps we can take to getting out from under the corporate state?" The answer is yes, absolutely! The reality is, it is relatively simple. It does take some study, understanding, and effort, but the truth is that it is simple.

The first thing to do is to change your political status. Each and every one of us has the right to choose who we are and what our political status is. Right now, 99 percent of Americans are corporate citizens of the municipality in Washington, DC, known as the UNITED STATES OF AMERICA, incorporated, that is owned by the Rothchilds and their international banking friends and families. All corporate citizens of the UNITED STATES OF AMERICA are identified by their name being in all capitalized letters on all of their government-issued documents. All of their banking documents and social security documents will also have their name in all capitals.

If this is your political status, you may keep this status if you choose, and you will have the benefits of the

STATE. If you decide you do not want the political status of a corporate citizen of the STATE, then you may change your political status to that of an American national.

There are several ways to do this; all of them require that you give public notice of who you are.

As I was studying on how to do this, I have done it several ways. The first way was to create an affidavit (see appendix E) under the penalty of perjury stating who I was as it relates to the Fourteenth Amendment. I went to file this affidavit in the local courthouse, and they refused to allow me to file it. Why may you ask would they not allow me to file this affidavit with the county clerk? The reason is, once this affidavit was of public record, it takes away the presumption that the courts have control and authority over our lives. By refusing to allow me to file this affidavit the county violated my rights. I intend to go after them at a later date. My next step is to file the affidavit in a neighboring county who obeys the law. I have used this affidavit in several court cases, and the judges and opposing attorneys eventually just wanted me to go away.

I also filed in the local newspaper the following affidavit for ten days as public notice.

Act of Expatriation, Domicile Declaration and Allegiance

Whereas Michael R. Blackwell and MICHAEL R. BLACKWELL and all similarly named vessels in trade or commerce are all naturalized "citizens of the United States" under the Diversity Clause and are the age of majority and whereas such citizenship was never desired nor intended nor willingly nor voluntarily entered into under conditions of full disclosure They/THEY willingly and purposefully renounce all citizenship or other assumed political status or obligation related to the United States defined as "the territories and District of Columbia" (13 Stat. 223, 306, ch. 173 sec. 182, June 30, 1864) and its government, a corporation doing business variously as the UNITED STATES, THE UNITED STATES OF AMERICA, District of Columbia Municipal Corporation, etc., and permanently domicile upon and repatriate to the soil of Their/ Their birth known as California and freely affirm Their/THEIR true nationality as American State Nationals and American State Vessels in all international and maritime commerce including all operations under Article X of The Constitution for the united State of America and Article X of The Constitution of the United States of America, owned and operated by Blackwell, Michael Ray c/o 3040 Oakshire Street, Denton, Texas 76209, c/o Post Office Box 51655, Denton, Texas, 76206. That I reserve my unalienable right to amend this Affidavit at times and place of my own choosing, according as new facts and revelations are made available to me at various future times and places as yet unknown, and as yet to be determined, given the massive fiscal fraud which has now been sufficiently revealed to me by means of material and other reliable evidence which constitutes satisfactory and incontrovertible proof of the fraud to which I refer to in this Affidavit. And further, That I affirm, under penalty of perjury, under the Common Law of America, without the "United States", under the laws of the United States of America that the foregoing is true and correct, to the best of my current information, knowledge, and belief, per 28 U.S.C. 1746(1).

"WITH EXPLICIT RESERVATION OF ALL MY RIGHTS AND WITHOUT PREJUDICE UCC 1-207 (UCCA 1207)" and I also express reservation of all my rights in law, equity and all other natures law.

This action I validate and affirm this 21th date of July, 2017. by Michael Ray Blackwell, all rights reserved.

NOTARY

Denton County Texas State

This 21th day of July 2017 did visit one living man known as Michael Ray Blackwell and he did establish this Act of Expatriation, Domicile and Allegiance freely and without coercion, in Witness whereof I set my sign and seal.

_____

Notary; my commission expires on _____.

Also, I filed some documents that Anna Von Reitz and her team created to remove all doubt about our political status and to take away any presumption that I am a corporate citizen of the UNITED STATES OF AMERICA INC. You may find Anna's editable documents at her website: http://www.annavonreitz.com/.

And the last thing I have done is join my county jural assembly in the Texas republic. I suggest you seek out your own county and state jural assembly and join and participate in them. A jural assembly is an unincorporated association of people who join together for the purpose of defining and enforcing local law. This is your lawful government, not the corporate state.

These are some steps that you may take, as many others have already taken, to restore your political status back to being a free man or woman according to law. The corporate government as described earlier, does not have any authority over a living man.

American state nationals are reassembling throughout every state of the union to reinstate our lawful government. Our lawful government is not lost; it has been in abeyance since 1861. According to the Lieber Code, Executive Order No. 100 signed by Abraham Lincoln, once the lawful government of the people is reassembled, the military courts, corporate government will shut down and cease to exist. All functions of government will continue but be operated by our lawful government of the people, by the people, and for the people as defined in the original US Constitution.

13

TO MY FELLOW AMERICANS

There is so much information available confirming the things I have been discussing with you. It is amazing. This information is available in plain sight, you just have to have the will to do the research. Here are some quotes I found about the propensity for theft, deceit and treason on a grand scale:

> History records that the money changers have used every form of abuse, intrigue, deceit, and violent means possible to maintain their control over governments by controlling money and its issuance.
>
> **—James Madison (1751-1836)**

> A theft of greater magnitude and still more ruinous, is the making of paper money; it is greater because in this money there is absolutely no real value; it is more ruinous because by its gradual depreciation

during the time of its existence, it produces the effect which would be proration of the coins. All those entities are founded on the false idea the money is but a sign.

—Count Destutt de Tracy, 1754-1836

If ever again our nation stumbles upon unfunded paper, it shall surely be like death to our body politic. This country will crash.

—George Washington (1732-1799)

If the American people ever allow private banks to control the issue of their currency, first by inflation, then by deflation, the banks . . . will deprive the people of all property until their children wake-up homeless on the continent their fathers conquered . . . The issuing power should be taken from the banks and restored to the people, to whom it properly belongs. . . . Paper is poverty. It is the ghost of money and not money itself.

—Thomas Jefferson (1743-1826)

The few who understand the system, will either be so interested from its profits or so dependent on its favors, that there will be no opposition from that class. . . . Let me issue and control a nation's money and I care not who writes the laws.

—Mayer Amschel Bauer Rothschild (1744-1812)

TO MY FELLOW VETERANS

You have served your country with honor and self-sacrifice. May God bless you all. I am proud of you and honored to have served with you.

I have a couple of questions for you? How do you think things are going in America these days? How do you think things are going internationally for America these days? These questions are not a Democratic or Republican issue, these questions are an American issue. These questions are not a politically left or politically right issue. These questions are an American issue.

The information that I have provided in this book was hard for me to accept. That being said, after forty-five years of trying to figure this out, I know it is a fact. I want to thank all of the American patriots who have worked hard to expose the truth. I am grateful.

When we joined the military, we all took an oath to "defend the Constitution against all enemies, foreign and domestic." As I have experienced life and grown in many ways, this oath has become more important to me. But the question I began to ask and I post to you, my fellow veterans, is what constitution did you swear an oath to? Did you swear allegiance to our original Constitution that was ratified in 1787 by our forefathers? Or did you promise to defend the constitution of 1871, which is basically a corporate charter of the municipality of Washington, District of Columbia? If it was the 1871 constitution, this is a privately owned corporation that is owned and controlled by the Rothchilds, their international banker friends and associates and satanists.

When I checked my DD-214, I saw my name spelled in all capital letters. Remember, this is not me, the living, flesh-and-blood man. It is the corporation that was created shortly after my birth by registering with the DEPARTMENT OF VITAL STATISTICS of the STATE OF CALIFORNIA. This corporation that is named after me, is a CITIZEN of the corporation created in 1871. This corporate citizen has PRIVILEGES, not God given rights protected by America's original founding documents.

Did you know this when you took your oath? I did not. I thought when I took the oath that I was swearing to protect the Constitution against all enemies, foreign and domestic, that this was the Constitution of our Founding Fathers. It turns out it was not.

As I began to understand what the truth was, I wondered if my friends who died or were maimed, wounded, or captured in Laos, Cambodia, North Vietnam and South Vietnam would have made those sacrifices if they knew and understood this truth: that they swore an oath to a private corporation, not our country. I think not. It is one of the reasons I decided to write this book. I simply wanted to expose the truth so that my fellow Americans may choose if they want to follow the truth or simply follow the lies and deceit. This is called intrinsic fraud. It is simply when there is a contract between two parties, and one does not disclose the full facts—the truth—to the other party. This is what has happened, and continues to happen, in America every day. I find this disgusting and evil.

So, looking at this fact in a spiritual sense, through spiritual eyes, what does this tell us? What does Scripture tell us? Satan is the father of all lies:

> You are of your father the devil, and the desires of your Father you want to do. He was a murderer from the beginning, and does not stand in the truth, because there is no truth in him. When he speaks the lie, he speaks it out of his own resources, for he is a liar and the father of it." **(John 8:44)**

We have a problem. Our forefathers gave us a republic per Benjamin Franklin. Yet everyone says we live in a democracy. Why? Which is it? It cannot be both can it? A republic is a state in which supreme power is held by the people and their elected representatives, and which has a nominated or elected President rather than a monarch. Democracy is tyranny of the majority, which is why the Founding Fathers gave us a Constitutional Republic. They feared that in a democracy, the majority would dominate and enslave the minority, or worse. Our founding documents including the original constitution was written by men who were familiar with God's Word and designed our government to reflect God's Word and to use American common law. Our founding documents limited government. Our founding documents made God sovereign and then ordered the power to American national citizens, then the counties, then the states, and finally the federal government. Is that what we have today? What happened? Maybe what I and others are trying to tell you is the truth.

> "You are near, O LORD And all Your commandments are truth. . . . The entirety of Your word is truth, And every one of Your righteous judgments endures forever" **(Psalm 119:151 and 160).**

The government we have today, the federal government claims it is sovereign first, then the states, then the counties, and then the people. God is not even allowed in our corporate government or corporate schools. Why is that? What happened? What is the spiritual nature of our government and schools today in America? Look at the facts through your spiritual eyes. Were we, the American people asleep, trusting our government, our representatives, our public servants, the main stream media? We better wake up and soon.

TO MY FELLOW CHRISTIANS

Could it be that the FBI undercover acquaintance of mine I described earlier is right? Could he be right about America's seminaries being infiltrated over a long period of time, just like our universities. Could it be that America's seminaries are not teaching the absolute Word of God? If this is true, each one of us better study the Word of God ourselves. Each one of us have a responsibility to study the Word of God. Are our preachers, pastors, laity, priests, or the Pope teaching the absolute Word of God? If you do not know, you better study and determine for yourselves.

Be diligent to present yourself approved to God, a worker who does not need to be ashamed, rightly dividing the word of truth. **(2 Timothy 2:15)**

You are of your father the devil, and the desires of your Father you want to do. He was a murderer from the beginning, and does not stand in the truth, because there is no truth in him. When he speaks the lie, he speaks it out of his own resources, for he is a liar and the father of it. **(John 8:44)**

The thief does not come except to steal and kill and destroy; I have come that they may have life, and that they may have it abundantly. **(John 10:10)**

You are near, O Lord And all of your commandments are truth. **(Psalm 119:151)**

The sum of your word is truth, And all Your righteous ordinances are forever. **(Psalm 119:16)**

Just by reviewing these few scriptures, we can determine that truth is important. That God is truth and operates in truth. Satan is a liar and the father of lies. These are polar opposites of the spectrum. There is no compromise. Truth is truth, and a lie is a lie.

> Now therefore fear Jehovah, and serve Him in sincerity and faithfulness: and put away the gods whom your fathers served across the River and in Egypt, and serve the Jehovah. And if it seems wrong in your sight to serve Jehovah, choose for yourselves today whom you will serve, either the gods from across the River whom your fathers served, or the gods of the Amorites, in whose land you dwell. But as for me and my household, we will serve Jehovah. (**Joshua 24:14-15**)

My fellow believers in Jesus, the Christ, we have a spiritual responsibility to seek the Lord. We have a spiritual responsibility to do the will of God, the God of Abraham, Issac, and Jacob who gave us his only begotten Son, Jesus Christ.

Have we, the American people been deceived?

Now, take a look at the spiritual nature of our founding documents. Are they based upon Scripture? Are they based on American common law?

Now, take a look at the spiritual nature of American government today. Take a look at the statutory law we have today. Statutory law is man's law. It is not God's law.

Is it operating under the constitution of 1787 or 1871? Is it operating based upon Scripture? Is it operating on American common law? Does the government lie, or deceive sometimes? Is the American government corrupt? Does the American government promote abortion? Truly, these questions could go on for a long time.

Are all the people working for government bad people? Absolutely not! Most of the people working for government are good people and a lot of them are patriots. Do they understand what I have been trying to explain to you? Probably not very many. They are Americans who were taught at the same schools, colleges, and universities as everyone else. They listen to the same media as everyone else. So, really, it is just an education process and then things will begin to change for the better.

Our lawyers do not disclose this to us. Why not? Our bankers do not disclose this to us. Why not?

When is a revival coming to America? I believe it is coming now! I have wanted revival to come to America for a long time. I always thought that other people needed to change. That they needed to return to the God of the Bible. I finally realized that revival and change needed to start with me. I started studying the Bible in earnest. Daily. The change in myself has been tremendous. It is the best thing I have ever done. This has been going on for ten plus years and will continue as long as I am able. I am thankful that God has given me this opportunity to grow spiritually.

So, what do you think? Has the Christian community been asleep while Satan has methodically changed our form of government? It is up to each one of us to figure things out. It is our individual responsibility.

What are you going to do?

TO AMERICA'S CLERGY

I have a couple of questions for you. Are you teaching *your* religion to your flock? Or are you teaching the absolute Word of God? Why are most churches today 501(c) corporations? When a church incorporates, it becomes the property of the government. A corporation is a dead corporation. A 501(c) corporation is subject to the government's admiralty courts and its rules and regulations. Why would you put the living God who is for living, breathing, flesh-and-blood men and women who have a body, spirit and soul under the authority of a dead entity that has a satanic nature?

You need to examine under whose authority you have placed your church and congregation. Are you under the authority and jurisdiction of the kingdom of the dead? Or are you under the authority and jurisdiction of the living Most High God as described in the Scriptures of the Holy Bible?

The time of choosing is now. Choose wisely, choose life.

To be continued . . .

APPENDIX A

Court Cases Regarding the Right to Travel

1. "The right of a citizen to travel upon the public highways and to transport his property thereon, by horse-drawn carriage, wagon or automobile, is not a mere privilege which may be permitted or prohibited at will, but a common right which he has under his right to life, liberty and the pursuit of happiness. Under this constitutional guaranty one may, therefore, under normal conditions, travel at his inclination along the public highways or in public places, and while conduction himself in an orderly and decent manner, neither interfering with nor disturbing another's rights, he will be protected, not only in his person, but in his safe conduct." (Thompson v Smith, 154 SE 579, 11 American Jurisprudence Constitutional Law, section 329, page 1135)

2. "The right of the Citizen to travel upon the public highways and to transport his

property thereon, in the ordinary course of life and business, is a common right which he has under the right to enjoy life and liberty, to acquire and possess property, and to pursue happiness and safety. It includes the right, in so doing, to use the ordinary and usual conveyances of the day, and under the existing modes of travel, includes the right to drive a horse drawn carriage or wagon thereon or to operate an automobile thereon, for the unusual and ordinary purpose of life and business." (Thompson v. Smith, supra,; Teche Lines v. Danforth, Miss., 12 S.2d 784)

3. "The right of the citizen to drive on a public street with freedom from police interference … is a fundamental constitutional right." (White. 97 Cal.App.3d.141, 158 Cal. Rptr.562.566-67, 1979)

4. "Citizens have a right to drive upon the public streets of the District of Columbia or any other city absent a constitutionally sound reason for limiting their access." (Cameisha Mills v. D.C., 2009)

5. "The use of the automobile as a necessary adjunct to the earning of a livelihood in modern life requires us in the interest of realism to conclude that the RIGHT to use an automobile on the public highways

partakes of the nature of a liberty within the meaning of the Constitutional guarantees." (Berberian v. Lussier, 1958, 139 A2d 869, 872; See also: Schecter v. Killingsworth, 380 P.2d 136, 140; 93 Ariz. 273, 1963).

6. "The right to operate a motor vehicle (an automobile) upon the public streets and highways is not a mere privilege. It is a right of liberty, the enjoyment of which is protected by the guarantees of the federal and state constitutions." (Adams v. Pocatello, 416 P.2d 46, 48; 91 Idaho 99, 1966)

7. "A traveler has an equal right to employ an automobile as a means of transportation and to occupy the public highways with other vehicles in common use." (Campbell v. Walker, 78 Alt. 601, 603, 2 Boyce, Del., 41)

8. "The owner of an automobile has the same right as the owner of other vehicles to use the highway, *** A traveler on foot has the same right to the use of the public highways as an automobile or any other vehicle." (Simeone v. Lindsay, 65 Alt. 778, 779; Hannigan v. Wright, 63 Atl. 234, 236)

9. "The right of the citizen to drive on the public street with freedom from police interference, unless he is engaged in

suspicious conduct associated in some manner with criminality is a fundamental constitutional right which must be protected by the courts." (People v. Horton 14 Cal. App. 3rd 667, 1971)

10. "The right to make use of an automobile as a vehicle of travel along the highways of the state, is no longer an open question. The owners thereof have the same rights in the roads and streets as the drivers of horses or those riding a bicycle or traveling in some other vehicle." (House v. Cramer, 112 N.W.3; 134 Iowa 374; Farnsworth v. Tampa Electric Co. 57 So. 233, 237, 62 Fla. 166)

11. "The automobile may be used with safety to other users of the highway, and in its proper use upon the highways there is an equal right with the users of other vehicles properly upon the highways. The law recognizes such right of use upon general principles." (Brinkman v. Pacholike, 84 N.E. 762, 764, 41 Ind. App 662, 666)

12. "The law does not denounce motor carriages, as such, on public ways. They have an equal right with other vehicles in common use to occupy the streets and roads. It is improper to say that the driver of the horse has rights in the roads superior

to the driver of the automobile. Both have the right to use the easement." (Indiana Springs Co. v. Brown. 165 Ind. 465, 468)

13. "A highway is a public way open and free to anyone who has occasion to pass along it on foot or with any kind of vehicle." (Schlesinger v. City of Atlanta 129 S.E. 861, 867, 161 Ga. 148, 159; Holland v. Shackelfor, 137 S.E. 2d 298, 304, 220 Ga. 104; Stavola v. Palmer, 73 A.2d 831, 838, 136 Conn. 670)

14. "There can be no question of the right of automobile owners to occupy and use the public streets of cities, or highways in the rural districts." (Liebrecht v. Crandall, 126 N.W. 69, 110 Minn. 454, 456)

15. "The word 'automobile' connotes a pleasure vehicle designed for the transportation of persons on highways." (American Mutual Liability Ins. Co. vs. Chaput, 60 A.2d 118, 120; 95 NH 200)

16. "The term 'motor vehicle' means every description of carriage or other contrivance propelled or drawn by mechanical power and used for commercial purposes on the highways ... The term 'used for commercial purposes' means the carriage of persons or property for any fare, fee, rate, charge or other consideration, or directly or

indirectly in connection with any business, or other undertaking intended for profit." (Motor Vehicle: 18 USC Part 1 Chapter 2 section 31 definitions: (6) "motor vehicle" and (10) "used for commercial purposes")

17. "A motor vehicle or automobile for hire is a motor vehicle, other than an automobile stage, used for the transportation of persons for which remuneration is received." (International Motor Transit Co. vs. Seattle , 251, p. 120)

18. "The term 'motor vehicle' is different and broader than the word 'automobile.'" (City of Dayton vs. DeBrose, 23 NE.2d 647, 650; 62 Ohio App 232)

19. "Thus self-driven vehicles are classified according to the use to which they are put rather than according to the means by which they are propelled." (Ex Parte Hoffert, 148 NW 20)

20. "The Supreme Court, in Arthur v. Morgan held that carriages were properly classified as household effects, and we see no reason that automobiles should not be similarly disposed of." (Hillhouse v. United States, 152 F. 163, 164, 2nd Cir. 1907)

21. "A citizen has the right to travel upon the public highways and to transport his property thereon." (State vs. Johnson, 243

P. 1073; Cummins vs. Homes, 155 P. 171; Packard vs. Banton, 44 S.Ct. 256; Hadfield vs. Lundin, 98 Wash 516. Willis vs. Buck, 263 P. 1982; Barney vs. Board of Railroad Commissioners, 17 P.2d 82)

22. "The use of the highways for the purpose of travel and transportation is not a mere privilege, but a common and fundamental right of which the public and the individual cannot be rightfully deprived." (Chicago Motor Coach vs. Chicago, 169 NE 22; Ligar vs. Chicago, 28 NE 934; Boon vs. Clark, 214 SSW 607; 25 Am.Jur., 1st Highways Sect.163)

23. "The right of the Citizen to travel upon the highway and to transport his property hereon in the ordinary course of life and business...is the usual and ordinary right of the Citizen, a right common to all." (Dickey vs. Davis, 85 SE 781)

24. "Every citizen has an unalienable right to make use of the public highways of the state; every citizen has full freedom to travel from place to place in the enjoyment of life and liberty." (People v. Nothaus, 147 Colo. 210)

25. "No state government entity has the power to allow or deny passage on the highways, byways, nor waterways . . . transporting

his vehicles and personal property for either recreation or business, but by being subject only to local regulation i.e., safety, caution, traffic lights, speed limits, etc. Travel is not a privilege requiring licensing, vehicle registration, or forced insurances." (Chicago Coach Co. v. City of Chicago, 337 Ill. 200, 169 N.E. 22)

26. "Traffic violations are not a crime." (People v. Battle)

27. "Persons faced with an unconstitutional licensing law which purports to require a license as a prerequisite to exercise of right…may ignore the law and engage with impunity in exercise of such right." (Shuttlesworth v. Birmingham 394 U.S. 147, 1969)

28. "The word 'operator' shall not include any person who solely transports his own property and who transports no persons or property for hire or compensation." (Statutes at Large California Chapter 412 p. 83)

29. "Highways are for the use of the traveling public, and all have the right to use them in a reasonable and proper manner: the use thereof is an inalienable right of every citizen." (Escobedo vs. State 35 C2d 870 in 8 Cal Jur 3d p. 27)

30. "Right --- A legal right, a constitutional right means a right protected by the law, by the constitution, but government does not create the idea of Right or original rights; it acknowledges them..." (Bouvier's Law Dictionary 1914, p. 2961)

31. "Those who have the right to do something cannot be licensed for what they already have right to do as such license would be meaningless." (City of Chicago v. Collins 51 NE 907, 910)

32. "A license means leave to do a thing which the licensor could prevent." (Blatz Brewing Co. v. Collins, 160 P.2d 37, 39; 69 Cal. A. 2d 639)

33. "The object of a license is to confer a right or power, which does not exist without it." (Payne v. Massey 119, 196 SW 2nd 493, 145 Tex 273)

34. "The court makes it clear that a license relates to qualifications to engage in profession, business, trade or calling; thus, when merely traveling without compensation or profit, outside of business enterprise or adventure with the corporate state, no license is required of the natural individual traveling for personal business, pleasure and transportation." (Wingfield v. Fielder 2d Ca. 3d 213, 1972)

35. "If state officials construe a vague statue unconstitutionally, the citizen may take them at their word, and act on the assumption that the statue is void." (Shuttlesworth v. Birmingham 394 U.S. 147, 1969)

36. "With regard particularly to the U.S. Constitution, it is elementary that a right secured or protected by that document cannot be overthrown or impaired by any state police authority." (Donnolly vs. Union Sewer Pipe Co., 184 US 540; Lafarier vs. Grand Trunk R.R. Co., 24 A. 884; O'Neil vs. Providence Amusement Co., 108 A. 887)

37. "The right to travel (called the right of free ingress to other states, and egress from them) is so fundamental that it appears in the Articles of Confederation, which governed our society before the Constitution." (Paul v. Virginia)

38. "The right to travel freely from State to State...is a right broad assertable against private interference as well as governmental action. Like the right of association, it is a virtually unconditional personal right, guaranteed by the Constitution to us all." (U.S. Supreme Court Shapiro v. Thompson)

39. Edgerton, Chief Judge: "Iron Curtains have no place in a free world..."Undoubtedly the right of locomotion, the right to remove from one place to another according to inclination, is an attribute of personal liberty, and the right, ordinarily, of free transit from or through the territory of any State is a right secured by the Constitution." (Williams v. Fears)

40. Our nation has thrived on the principle that, outside areas of plainly harmful conduct, every American is left to shape his own life as he thinks best, do what he pleases. Go where he pleases." (Ad., at 197, Kent vs. Dulles see Vestal, Freedom of Movement, 41 Iowa L.Rev.6. 13-14)

41. "The validity of restrictions on the freedom of movement of particular individuals, both substantively and procedurally, is precisely the sort of matter that is the peculiar domain of the courts." (Comment, 61 Yale I.J. at page 187)

42. "a person detained for an investigatory stop can be questioned but is "not obligated to answer, answers may not be compelled, and refusal to answer furnishes no basis for an arrest." (Justice White Hibe)

43. "Automobiles have the right to use the highways of the State on an equal footing

with other vehicles." (Cumberland Telephone & Telegraph Co. v. Yeiser 141 Kentucky 15)

44. "Each citizen has the absolute right to choose for himself the mode of conveyance he desires, whether it be by wagon or carriage, by horse, motor or electric car, or by bicycle, or astride of a horse, subject to the sole condition that he will observe all those requirements that are known as the law of the road. (Swift v. City of Topeka, 43)

45. The Supreme Court said, "An administrative regulation, of course, is not a "statute." (U.S. v. Mersky, 1960, 361 U.S. 431)

46. "A traveler on foot has the same right to use of the public highway as an automobile or any other vehicle." (Cecchi v. Lindsay, 75 Atl. 376, 377, 1 Boyce, Del., 185)

47. "Automotive vehicles are lawful means of conveyance and have equal rights upon the streets with horses and carriages." (Chicago Coach Co. v. City of Chicago, 337 Ill. 200, 205; See also: Christy v. Elliot, 216 Ill. 31; Ward v. Meredith, 202 Ill. 66; Shinkle v. McCullough, 116 Ky. 960; Butler v. Cabe, 116 Ark. 26, 28-29)

48. "Automobiles are lawful vehicles and have equal rights on the highways with horses

and carriages." (Daily v. Maxwell, 133
S.W. 351, 354. Matson v. Dawson, 178
N.W. 2d 588, 591)

49. "A farmer has the same right to the use of
the highways of the state, whether on foot
or in a motor vehicle, as any other citizen."
(Daffin v. Massey, 92 S.E.2d, 38, 42)

50. "Persons may lawfully ride in automobiles,
as they may lawfully ride on bicycles."
(Doherty v. Ayer, 83 N.E. 677, 197 Mass.
241, 246; Molway v. City of Chicago, 88
N.E. 485, 486, 239 Ill. 486; Smiley v. East
St. Louis Ry. Co., 100 N.E. 157, 158)

APPENDIX B

THE NAKED COMMUNIST: 45 COMMUNIST GOALS

On January 10, 1963, Congressman Albert S. Herlong Jr. of Florida read a list of forty-five Communist goals into the Congressional Record. The list was derived from researcher Cleon Skousen's book *The Naked Communist*. These principles are well worth revisiting today in order to gain insights into the thinking and strategies of much of our so-called liberal elite:

1. U.S. should accept coexistence as the only alternative to atomic war.
2. U.S. should be willing to capitulate in preference to engaging in atomic war.
3. Develop the illusion that total disarmament by the U.S. would be a demonstration of "moral strength."
4. Permit free trade between all nations regardless of Communist affiliation and regardless of whether or not items could be used for war.
5. Extend long-term loans to Russia and Soviet satellites.

6. Provide American aid to all nations regardless of Communist domination.

7. Grant recognition of Red China and admission of Red China to the U.N.

8. Set up East and West Germany as separate states in spite of Khrushchev's promise in 1955 to settle the Germany question by free elections under supervision of the U.N.

9. Prolong the conferences to ban atomic tests because the U.S. has agreed to suspend tests as long as negotiations are in progress.

10. Allow all Soviet satellites individual representation in the U.N.

11. Promote the U.N. as the only hope for mankind. If its charter is rewritten, demand that it be set up as a one-world government with its own independent armed forces.

12. Resist any attempt to outlaw the Communist Party.

13. Do away with loyalty oaths.

14. Continue giving Russia access to the U.S. Patent Office.

15. Capture one or both of the political parties in the U.S.

16. Use technical decisions of the courts to weaken basic American institutions, by claiming their activities violate civil rights.

17. Get control of the schools. Use them as transmission belts for Socialism and

current Communist propaganda. Soften the curriculum. Get control of teachers associations. Put the party line in textbooks.

18. Gain control of all student newspapers.

19. Use student riots to foment public protests against programs or organizations that are under Communist attack.

20. Infiltrate the press. Get control of book review assignments, editorial writing, policy-making positions.

21. Gain control of key positions in radio, TV & motion pictures.

22. Continue discrediting American culture by degrading all form of artistic expression.

23. Control art critics and directors of art museums. " Our plan is to promote ugliness, repulsive, meaningless art."

24. Eliminate all laws governing obscenity by calling them "censorship" and a violation of free speech and free press.

25. Break down cultural standards of morality by promoting pornography and obscenity in books, magazines, motion pictures, radio and TV.

26. Present homosexuality, degeneracy and promiscuity as "normal, natural and healthy

27. Infiltrate the churches and replace revealed religion with "social" religion. Discredit the Bible and emphasize the need for

intellectual maturity, which does not need a "religious crutch."

28. Eliminate prayer or any phase of religious expression in the schools on the grounds that it violates the principle of "separation of church and state"

29. Discredit the American Constitution by calling it inadequate, old fashioned, out of step with modern needs, a hindrance to cooperation between nations on a worldwide basis.

30. Discredit the American founding fathers. Present them as selfish aristocrats who had no concern for the "common man."

31. Belittle all forms of American culture and discourage the teaching of American history on the ground that it was only a minor part of "the big picture." Give more emphasis to Russian history since the Communists took over.

32. Support any socialist movement to give centralized control over any part of the culture – education, social agencies, welfare programs, mental health clinics, etc.

33. Eliminate all laws or procedures which interfere with the operation of the Communist apparatus.

34. Eliminate the House Committee on Un-American Activities.

35. Discredit and eventually dismantle the FBI.
36. Infiltrate and gain control of more unions.
37. Infiltrate and gain control of big business.
38. Transfer some of the powers of arrest from the police to social agencies. Treat all behavioral problems as psychiatric disorders which no one but psychiatrists can understand or treat.
39. Dominate the psychiatric profession and use mental health laws as a means of gaining coercive control over those who oppose communist goals.
40. Discredit the family as an institution. Encourage promiscuity and easy divorce.
41. Emphasize the need to raise children away from the negative influence of parents. Attribute prejudices, mental blocks and retarding of children to suppressive influence of parents.
42. Create the impression that violence and insurrection are legitimate aspects of the American tradition; that students and special interest groups should rise up and make a "united force" to solve economic, political or social problems.
43. Overthrow all colonial governments before native populations are ready for self-government.

44. Internationalize the Panama Canal.

45. Repeal the Connally Reservation so the U.S. cannot prevent the World Court from seizing jurisdiction over domestic problems. Give the World Court jurisdiction over domestic problems. Give the World Court jurisdiction over nations and individuals alike.

APPENDIX C

JURISDICTION COURT CASES

"We acknowledged that "the immunity of a truly independent sovereign from suit in its own courts has been enjoyed as a matter of absolute rights for centuries. Only the sovereign's own consent could qualify the absolute attribute of sovereignty is reflected in our cases," id at 415, and that "this explanation adequately supports the conclusion that no sovereign may be sued in its own courts without its consent." [Id., at 416. ALDEN v. MAINE, 527 U.S. 706 (1999)(2). Justice KENNEDY (Supreme Court of the United States)]

Chief Justice Jay took a less vehement tone in his opinion, but he, too, denied the applicability of the doctrine of sovereign immunity to the States. He explained the doctrine as an incident of European feudalism, and said that by contrast, "no such ideas obtain here: at the Revolution, the sovereignty devolved on the people; and they are truly the sovereigns of the country, but they are sovereigns without subjects (unless the African slaves among us may be so called) and have none to govern but themselves; the citizens of America are equal as fellow citizens, and as joint tenants in the sovereignty." [ALDEN v. MAINE, 527 U.S. 706 (1999)(2). Justice SOUTER (Supreme Court of the United States) STEVENS,GINSBURG, and Justice BREYER join, dissenting]

"The laws of Congress in respect to those matters do not extend into the territorial limits of the states, but have force only in the District of Columbia, and other places that are within the exclusive jurisdiction of the national government." [Catha v United States, 152 US, at 215]

"Once jurisdiction is challenged, the court cannot proceed when it clearly appears that the court lacks jurisdiction, the court has no authority to reach merits, but, rather, should dismiss the action." [Melo v. US, 505 F2d 1026]

"The law requires proof of jurisdiction to appear on the record of the administrative agency and all administrative proceedings." [Hagans v Lavine, 415 U. S. 533]]

If you read the Supreme Court cases you will find that jurisdiction can be challenged at any time.

If it [jurisdiction] doesn't exist, it cannot justify conviction or judgment. ...without which power (jurisdiction) the state CANNOT be said to be "sovereign." At best, to proceed would be in "excess" of jurisdiction which is as well fatal to the State's/USA's cause. [Broom v. Douglas, 75 Ala 268, 57 So 860 the same being jurisdictional facts FATAL to the government's cause (e.g. see In re FNB, 152 F 64)]

"A judgment rendered by a court without personal jurisdiction over the defendant is void. It is a nullity. [A judgment shown to be void for lack of personal service on the defendant is a nullity.]" [Sramek v. Sramek, 17 Kan. App. 2d 573, 576-77, 840 P.2d 553 (1992), rev. denied 252 Kan. 1093 (1993)]"

A court cannot confer jurisdiction where none existed and cannot make a void proceeding valid. It is clear and well-established law that a void order can be challenged in any court" [OLD WAYNE_MUT.,_L. ASSOC, V. McDONOUGH, 204 U. S. 8, 27 S. Ct. 236 (1907)]

"There is no discretion to ignore lack of jurisdiction." [Joyce v. U.S. 474 2D 215]

"Court must prove on the record, all jurisdiction facts related to the jurisdiction asserted." [Latang v. Hopper, 102 F. 2d 188; Chicago v. New York 37 F Supp. 150]

"The law provides that once State and Federal Jurisdiction has been challenged, it must be proven." [Main v. Thiboutot, 100 S. Ct. 2502 (1980)]

"Jurisdiction can be challenged at any time." and "Jurisdiction, once challenged, cannot be assumed and must be decided." [Basso v. Utah Power & Light Co, 495 F 2d 906, 910]

"Defense of lack of jurisdiction over the subject matter may be raised at any time, even on appeal." [Rill Top Developers v. Holiday Pines Service Corp,, 478 So. 2d. 368 (Fla 2nd DCA 1985)]

"Once challenged, jurisdiction cannot be assumed, it must be proved to exist." [Stuck v. Medical Examiners 94 Ca 2d 751. 211 P2d 389]

"There is no discretion to ignore that lack of jurisdiction." [Joyce v. US, 474 F2d 215]

"The burden shifts to the court to prove jurisdiction." [Rosemond v. Lambert, 469 F2d 416]

"A universal principle as old as the law is that proceedings of a court without jurisdiction are a nullity and its judgment therein without effect either on person or property." [Norwood v. Renfield, 34 C 329; Ex parte Giambonini, 49 p. 732]

"Jurisdiction is fundamental and a judgment rendered by a court that does not have jurisdiction to hear is void ab initio." [In Re Application of Wyatt, 300 P. 132; Re Cavitt, 118 P2d 846]

"Thus, where a judicial tribunal has no jurisdiction of the subject matter on which it assumes to act, its proceedings are absolutely void in the fullest sense of the term." [Dillon v. Dillon, 187 p. 27]

"A court has no jurisdiction to determine its own jurisdiction, for a basic issue in any case before a tribunal is its power to act, and a court must have the authority to decide that question in the first instance." [Rescue Army v. Municipal Court of Los Angeles, 171 P2d 8; 331 US 549, 91 L. ed. 1666, 67 S.Ct. 1409]

"A departure by a court from those recognized and established requirements of law, however close apparent adherence to mere form in method of procedure, which has the effect of depriving one of a constitutional right, is an excess of jurisdiction." [Wuest v. Wuest, 127 P2d 934, 937]

"Where a court failed to observe safeguards, it amounts to denial of due process of law, court is deprived of juris." [Merritt v. Hunter C.A. Kansas 170 F2d 739]

"the fact that the petitioner was released on a promise to appear before a magistrate for an arraignment, that fact is circumstance to be considered in determining whether in first instance there was a probable cause for the arrest." [Monroe v. Papa, DC, Ill. 1963, 221 F Supp 6]

"We (judges) have no more right to decline the exercise of jurisdiction which is given, than to usurp that which is not given. The one or the other would be treason to the Constitution." [Cohen v. Virginia, (1821), 6 Wheat. 264 and U.S. v. Will, 499 U.S. 200]

APPENDIX D

SCRIPTURE REGARDING AUTHORITY

"Let every soul be subject to the governing authorities. For there is no authority except from God, and the authorities that exist are appointed by God." **(Romans 13:1)**

"Forever, O Lord, Your word is settled in heaven." **(Psalm 119:89)**

"This book of the law shall not depart from your mouth, but you shall meditate in it day and night, that you may observe to do according to all that is written in it. For then you will make your way prosperous and then you will have success." **(Joshua 1:8)**

"Therefore be very courageous to keep and do all that is written in the book of the law of Moses, lest you turn aside from it to the right or to the left." **(Joshua 23:6)**

"The grass withers, the flower fades, But the word of our God will stand forever." **(Isaiah 40:8)**

"Do not think that I have come to abolish the law or the prophets; I did not come to destroy, but to fulfill." **(Matthew 5:17)**

"For assuredly, I say to you, till heaven and earth pass away, one jot or one tittle will by no means pass from the law till all is fulfilled." **(Matthew 5:18)**

"Whoever therefore breaks one of the least of these commandments, and teaches men so, shall be called the least in the kingdom of the heaven; but whoever does and teaches them, he shall be called great in the kingdom of the heaven." **(Matthew 5:19)**

"And it is easier for heaven and earth to pass away than for one tittle of the law to fail." **(Luke 16:17)**

"For this reason we also thank God unceasing, because when you received the word of God, which you heard from us, you welcomed it not as the word of men, but as it is in truth, the word of God, which also effectively works in you who believe." **(1 Thessalonians 2:13)**

"And Jesus came and spoke to them, saying, All authority has been given to Me in heaven and on earth." **(Matthew 28:18)**

"Go therefore and make disciples of all the nations, baptizing them into the name of the Father and of the Son and of the Holy Spirit," **(Matthew 28:19)**

"And what is the exceeding greatness of His power toward us who believe, according to the working of his mighty power," **(Ephesians 1:19)**

"Which He worked in Christ when he raised Him from the dead and seated Him at His right hand in the heavenly places," **(Ephesians 1:20)**

"Far above all principality and power and might and dominion, and every name that is named, not only in this age but also in that which is to come. **(Ephesians 1:21)**

"And He put all things under His feet, and gave Him to be head over all things to the church." **(Ephesians 1:22)**

"Which is His Body, the fullness of Him who fills all in all." **(Ephesians 1:23)**

APPENDIX E

AFFIDAVIT REGARDING CITIZENSHIP

COUNTY OF DENTON
STATE OF TEXAS

I, Michael Blackwell, being of sound mind and lawful age, do solemnly declare:

1. I was born in CALIFORNIA State of parents who were white, who were citizen-principals and whose parents time out of mind were and always had been white. And as a hereditament I acquired directly and immediately the status of citizen-principal of said state sharing equally in its sovereignty.

2. The U.S. Supreme Court in the **Slaughter-House cases**, among other things stated:
It had been said by the eminent judges that no man was a citizen of the United States except as he was a citizen of one of the states composing the union. Those, therefore, who had been born and always resided in the District of Columbia or in

the territories, though within the United States, were not citizens. Whether this proposition was sound or not had never been judicially decided. But it had been held by this court, in the celebrated **Dred Scott cases,** only a few years before the outbreak of the civil war, that a man of African descent, whether slave or not, was not and could not be a citizen of a state or of the Untied States ... This decision ... had never been overruled; and, if was to be accepted as a constitutional limitation to citizenship, then all of the Negro race who had been recently made Freemen were still not only not citizens, but were incapable of becoming so by anything short of an amendment to the constitution.

To remove this difficulty primarily ... the 1st clause of the 1st section of the 14th amendment was framed ... that its main purpose was to establish the citizenship of the negro can admit no doubt ...

The next observation (respecting the first clause) ... is that the distinction between citizenship of the United States and the citizenship of a state is clearly recognized and established ...

It is quite clear, then, there is a citizenship of the United States and a citizenship of a state, which are distinct from each other and which depend upon different characteristics or circumstances in the individual ...

We think this distinction and its explicit recognition in the Amendment of great weight in this argument, because the next paragraph in the same section ... speaks only of privileges and immunities of citizens of the United States, and does not speak of those of the several states.

The language is: "No state shall make or enforce any law which shall abridge the privileges or immunities of the United States ... it is a little remarkable, if this clause was intended as a protection of the citizens of a state against the legislative power of his own state, that the words, "citizen of the state" should be left out when it is so carefully used in contradiction of "citizens of the United States in the very sentence which preceded it. It is too clear for argument that the change in phraseology was adopted understandingly and with a purpose.

Of the privileges and immunities of the citizens of the United States and of the privileges and immunities of the citizens of a state ... it is only the former which are placed by this clause (the second clause of the 14th Amendment) under the protection of the Federal Constitution, and that the latter, whatever they may be, are not intended to have any additional protection by this paragraph of the Amendment ... the latter must rest for their security and protection were they have heretofore rested, for they are not embraced by this paragraph of the Amendment.

But with ... exceptions ... few ... the entire domain of the privileges and immunities of citizens of the state, as above defined, **lay within the constitutional and legislative power of state,** and **without that of the Federal government.** Was it the purpose of the 14th Amendment ... to transfer the security and protection of all the civil rights which we have mentioned from the states to the Federal government? And ... that congress shall have ... the entire domain of civil rights heretofore belonging exclusively to the states?... (Emphasis added)

We are convinced that no such results were intended by the Congress which proposed these amendments, nor by the legislature of the states, which ratified them ..

Having shown that the privileges and immunities relied on in the argument are those which belong to citizens of the states as such, and that they are left to the state government ... we may hold ourselves excused from defining the privileges and immunities of citizens of the United States which no state can abridge, until some case involving those privileges may make it necessary to do so.

Slaughter-House cases 83 U.S. (16Wall) 36, 21 L.ED 394, 407-409 (1873).

3. The Supreme Court in United States v Wong Kim Ark, among other things stated: Chief Justice Waite said: "Allegiance and protection are, in this connection (that is, in relationship to citizenship) reciprocal obligations. The one is the compensation for the other, allegiance for protection, and protection for allegiance." At Common Law, with the nomenclature with which the framers of the constitution were familiar, it was never doubted that all children born in a country, of parents who were citizens, become themselves, upon their birth, citizens also ..." **Minor v Happepsett (1874) 21 Wall 162-168 ...**

United States v Wong Kim Ark 18 5.ct. 456, 468-469 (1898), and where there is no protection or allegiance or sovereignty there can be no claim to obedience. **4 Wheat 254.**

Id. 470, and the opening sentence of the fourteenth amendment is throughout affirmative and declaratory, intended to allay doubts and to settle controversies which had arisen, **and not to impose any new restrictions on citizenship. (Emphasis added)**

Id. 471, and further Mr. Justice Fuller in his dissenting opinion stated: At that time the theory largely obtained, as stated by Mr. Justice Story, in his commentaries on the Constitution (section 1693), "That every citizen of a state is **ipso facto** a citizen of the United States."

Id. 482

4. Based upon the above considerations and my other studies and deliberations and being under no duress, coercion, promise of reward or gain, or undue influence I have of my own free will determined it is clear from the opinions of the Supreme Court that prior to the 14th Amendment a white citizen of any of the several states ipso facto, derivative and mediate of his state citizenship, was a Citizen of the United States, that is, one of the principals of the political association identified as the

United States of America;

5. And as the 14th Amendment did **"not ... impose any new restrictions on citizenship all white men born in any of the several states,"** of parents who were its citizens, become them-selves, upon their birth, citizens also," and are "not intended to have any additional protection by the 14th Amendment.";

6. And because a white man's citizenship was not restricted by the 14th Amendment and because he receives no protection from it, he has no reciprocal obligation to a 14th Amendment allegiance or sovereignty and owes no obedience to anyone under the 14th Amendment.

7. And indeed it is a manifest fact observed by the Supreme Court that it was not any sovereignty (politically free will) with the black man, the states, or the United States that granted the citizenship established in the 14th Amendment: rather, it was the sovereignty in "the voice of the people." **Slaughter-House Cases, supra, at 406;**

8. And the people did not intend the 14th Amendment "as a protection of the citizen of a state against the legislative power of his own state";

9. And by my birth I am a free citizen of

the aforesaid state of my birth and a derivative and mediate thereof I am also a Citizen of the United States of America as contemplated in the Constitutional Contract of 1787;

10. I am not a citizen of the United States as contemplated by the 14th Amendment and that I do not reside in any state with the intention of receiving from the Federal government or any other party a protection against the legislative power of the state pursuant to the authority of the 14th Amendment;

11. And, therefore, I am 'non resident' to the residency and 'alien' to the citizenship of the 14th Amendment and, in the terminology of the Internal Revenue Code, I am 'nonresident alien individual' and subject to taxation imposed under Section 871 of the Code;

12. And as the tax imposed in 26 U.S.C. 1, pursuant to 26 C.F.R. 1.1-1, is on citizens and residents as contemplated by the 14th Amendment, it is not an applicable internal Revenue Law to me, as I am neither such a citizen or resident.

13. And with respect to an election under 26 U.S.C. 871(d) I have never knowingly, willingly, nor with my informed consent

voluntarily mad such an election. Notwithstanding the fact that I may have in past years filed form 1040 U.S. Individual Income Tax Returns, such filing were done in mistake by me not knowing that such filing were and are mandated only on citizens and residents of the United States as contemplated by the 14th Amendment. Furthermore, such filings were done by me with no knowledge that such filing would, or could, be construed to constitute an election under 26 U.S.C. 871 (d).

14. Furthermore, I am not a resident of any state under the 14th Amendment and hereby publicly disavow any contract, form, agreement, application, certificate, license, permit or other document that I or any other person may have signed expressly or by acquiescence that would grant me any privileges and thereby ascribe to m rights and duties under a substantive system of law other than that of the Constitutional Contract of 1787 for the United States and of the constitutions for the several States of the Union, exclusive of the 14th Amendment.

15. I reiterate that I have made the above determinations and this declaration under no duress, coercion, promise of reward or

gain, or undue influence of my free will, with no mental reservation.

16. I sincerely invite any person who has any reason to know or believe that I am in error in my determinations and conclusions above to inform me and to state the reason(s) they believe I am in error in writing at the location of my abode shown below.

17. That this is to certify that I, michael blackwell, am a Sovereign natural born free American National and inhabitant in the United States of America, domiciled in the Texas state, living on the land and in peace in Denton County, living under the Common Law, having assumed, among the powers of the Earth, the Separate and Equal Station to which the Laws of Nature and Nature's God entitles me, in order to secure the Blessings of Liberty to Myself and my Posterity, and in order to re-acquire the Birthright that was taken from me by the fraud, do hereby asseverate *nunc pro tunc* and rescind, *ab initio,* all feudatory contracts with the Federal government and its agencies, and with the corporate State of Texas and its agencies; for I, Michael Blackwell, being of sound mind and body, do not choose, nor have I ever chosen, to

give up, relinquish, or otherwise waive any of my God-given, natural, fundamental, Constitutional secured rights. And further,

18. That my use of the phrase "WITH EXPLICIT RESERVATION OF ALL MY RIGHTS AND WITHOUT PREJUDICE UCC 1-207 (UCCA 1207)" above my signature on this document indicates: (1) that I explicitly reject any and all benefits of the Uniform Commercial Code, absent a valid commercial agreement which is in force and to which I am a party, and cite its provisions herein only to serve notice upon ALL agencies of government, whether international, national, state or local, that they, and not I, are subject to, and bound by, all of its provisions, whether cited herein or not; (2) that my explicit reservation of rights has served notice upon ALL agencies of government of the "Remedy" they must provide for me under Article I, Section 207, of the Uniform Commercial Code, whereby I have explicitly reserved my Common Law right not to be compelled to perform under any contract or commercial agreement into which I have not entered knowingly, voluntarily, and intentionally, (3) that my explicit reservation of rights has served notice upon ALL agencies of

government that they are ALL limited to proceeding against me only in harmony with the Common Law and that I do not, and will not accept the liability associated with the "compelled" benefit of any unrevealed commercial agreements; and (4) that my valid reservation of rights has preserved all my rights and prevented the loss of any such rights by application of the concepts of waiver or estoppel. And further,

19. That I reserve my unalienable right to amend this Affidavit at times and place of my own choosing, according as new facts and revelations are made available to me at various future times and places as yet unknown, and as yet to be determined, given the massive fiscal fraud which has now been sufficiently revealed to me by means of material and other reliable evidence which constitutes satisfactory and incontrovertible proof of the fraud to which I refer in this paragraph and elsewhere in the Affidavit. And further,

20. That I affirm, under penalty of perjury, under the Common Law of America, without the "United States", under the laws of the United States *of America* that the foregoing is true and correct, to the best of

my current information, knowledge, and belief, per 28 U.S.C. 1746(1).

21. "WITH EXPLICIT RESERVATION OF ALL MY RIGHTS AND WITHOUT PREJUDICE UCC 1-207 (UCCA 1207)"

22. That I, Michael Blackwell, am a live, living, breathing, flesh and blood man, non- person, non-resident and alien as respect to the 14th Amendment, who is an American National living on the land in peace in Texas state. I am not a corporation or defacto.

That this is to certify that I, michael blackwell, am a Sovereign natural born free American National and inhabitant in the United States of America, domiciled in the Texas state, living on the land and in peace in Denton County, living under the Common Law, having assumed, among the powers of the Earth, the Separate and Equal Station to which the Laws of Nature and Nature's God entitles me, in order to secure the Blessings of Liberty to Myself and my Posterity, and in order to re-acquire the Birthright that was taken from me by the fraud, do hereby asseverate *nunc pro tunc* and rescind, *ab initio,* all feudatory contracts with the Federal government and its agencies, and with the corporate State of Texas and its agencies; for I, Michael Blackwell, being of sound mind and body, do not choose, nor have I ever chosen, to give up, relinquish, or otherwise waive any of my God-given, natural, fundamental, Constitutional secured rights. And further,

That my use of the phrase "WITH EXPLICIT RESERVATION OF ALL MY RIGHTS AND WITHOUT PREJUDICE UCC 1-207 (UCCA 1207)" above my signature on this document indicates: (1) that I explicitly reject any and all benefits of the Uniform Commercial Code, absent a valid commercial agreement which is in force and to which I am a party, and cite its provisions herein only to serve notice upon ALL agencies of government, whether international, national, state or local, that they, and not I, are subject to, and bound by, all of its provisions, whether cited herein or not; (2) that my explicit reservation of rights has served notice upon ALL agencies of government of the "Remedy" they must provide for me under Article I, Section 207, of the Uniform Commercial Code, whereby I have explicitly reserved my Common Law right not to be compelled to perform under any contract or commercial agreement into which I have not entered knowingly, voluntarily, and intentionally, (3) that my explicit reservation of rights has served notice upon ALL agencies of government that they are ALL limited to proceeding against me only in harmony with the Common Law and that I do not, and will not accept the liability associated with the "compelled" benefit of any unrevealed commercial agreements; and (4) that my valid reservation of rights has preserved all my rights and prevented the loss of any such rights by application of the concepts of waiver or estoppel. And further,

That I reserve my unalienable right to amend this Affidavit at times and place of my own choosing, according as new facts and revelations are made available to me at various future times and places as yet unknown, and as yet to be determined, given the massive fiscal fraud which has now been sufficiently revealed to me by means of material and other reliable evidence which constitutes satisfactory and incontrovertible proof of the fraud to which I refer in this paragraph and elsewhere in the Affidavit. And further,

That I affirm, under penalty of perjury, under the Common Law of America, without the "United States", under the laws of the United States *of America* that the foregoing is true and correct, to the best of my current information, knowledge, and belief, per 28 U.S.C. 1746(1).

"WITH EXPLICIT RESERVATION OF ALL MY RIGHTS AND WITHOUT PREJUDICE UCC 1-207 (UCCA 1207)" and I also express reservation of all my rights in law, equity and all other natures law.

Date: December 2, 2016

Michael Blackwell c/o _____

_____

_____

JURAT
State of Texas
County of Denton

Subscribed and sworn to (or affirmed) before me
on this 2nd day of December 2016 by Michael
Blackwell proved to me on the basis of satisfactory
evidence to be the person who appeared before
me.

Signature:_____ (Seal)
Notary Public

APPENDIX F

CRIMES AGAINST THE AMERICAN PEOPLE

1. **Identify Theft:** Deliberately obtaining and taking away someone else's personal information for criminal intentions.
2. **Fraud:** Deceitful practice or willful device, resorted to with intent to deprive another of his right, or in some manner to do him an injury.
3. **Constructive Fraud:** (1) An unintended deception, (2) Getting legal advantage through unfair means. The poor, the ignorant and the weak are targeted. The court may set aside the agreement due to the unreasonable terms of the contract.
4. **Fraud in the Inducement:** A phrase used when a person is tricked into signing a document.
5. **Legal Fraud:** The name given to the actions that are meant to mislead and deceive that may not have been in the original intent.
6. **Material Fraud:** The term that is applied

to tricking a person to enter a contract or agreement that without that trickery they wouldn't have considered.

7. **Moral Fraud:** The term given to the term of a wrong in a moral nature.

8. **Fraud in Treaty:** Where deceit is used to get a person to sign a document that will misrepresent the intended agreement.

9. **Dolus:** A fraudulent addressor trick used to deceive someone.

10. **Actionable Fraud:** Deception practiced in order to induce another to part with property or surrender some legal right; a false representation made with an intention to deceive; may be committed by stating what is known to be false or by professing knowledge of the truth of a statement which is false, but in either case, the essential ingredient is a falsehood uttered with intent to deceive.

11. **Fraud Ring:** An organization focused to defraud people. Forgery, false claims, stealing identities, counterfeiting checks and currencies are all fraudulent activities.

12. **Deceit:** A fraudulent and cheating misrepresentation, artifice, or device, used by one or more persons to deceive and trick another, who is ignorant of the true facts, to the prejudice and damage of the party

imposed upon.

13. **Fraudulent Act:** An act that has been with bad faith and dishonesty.

14. **Fraudulent Misrepresentation:** False statement. (1) intentional disregard of false or possibly false information, (2) falsely entering into a contract, and (3) causing loss based on false data leading to a contract.

15. **Fraudulent Concealment:** Intent to deceive or defraud in a contractual arrangement by deliberate hiding, nondisclosure, or suppression of a material fact or circumstance legally or morally bound to reveal. Also refer to suppression of evidence. Destruction, withholding or concealment, refusal to hand over evidence in your possession that you know you are morally or legally bound for you to reveal. 2. Court ruling where evidence is excluded from the trial because it was obtained illegally.

16. **Legal Malice:** the term used to describe the intentional performance to do a wrongful act. There is constructive malice, malice in law.

17. **Equitable Fraud:** Taking unfair, illegal advantage of disability, ignorance, or weakness.

18. **Unjust and discriminatory practices** by Title 28 U.S.C. officers, (judicial officers) for unlawful enrichment.

19. **Conspiracy against rights** is a federal offense in the United States of America under 18 U.S.C. §241:If two or more persons conspire to injure, oppress, threaten, or intimidate any person [...] in the free exercise or enjoyment of any right or privilege secured to him by the Constitution or laws of the United States, or because of his having so exercised the same;...or If two or more persons go in disguise on the highway, or on the premises of another, with intent to prevent or hinder his free exercise or enjoyment of any right or privilege so secured... They shall be fined under this title or imprisoned not more than ten years, or both; and if death results from the acts committed in violation of this section or if such acts include kidnapping or an attempt to kidnap, aggravated sexual abuse or an attempt to commit aggravated sexual abuse, or an attempt to kill, they shall be fined under this title or imprisoned for any term of years or for life, or both, or may be sentenced to death.

20. **Deprivation of rights under color of law:** Whoever, under color of any law, statute,

ordinance, regulation, or custom, willfully subjects any person in any State, Territory, Commonwealth, Possession, or District to the deprivation of any rights, privileges, or immunities, secured or protected by the Constitution or laws of the United States, or to different punishments, pains, or penalties for the punishment of citizens, shall be fined under this title or imprisoned not more than one year, or both, and if bodily injury results from the acts committed in violation of the section or if such acts include the use, attempted use, or threatened use of a dangerous weapon, explosives, or if such acts include the use, attempted use, or threatened use of a dangerous weapon, explosives, or fire, shall be fined under this title or imprisoned not more than ten years, or both, and if death results from the acts committed in violation of this section or if such acts include kidnapping or an attempt to kidnap, aggravated sexual abuse, or an attempt to commit aggravated sexual abuse, or an attempt to kill, shall be fined under this title, or imprisoned for any term of years or for life, or both, or may be sentenced to death.

21. **Fraud by deception** in denying human and constitutionally protected rights.
22. **Racketeering:** The Racketeer Influenced and Corrupt Organizations Act, commonly referred to as the RICO Act or simply RICO, is a United States federal law that provides for extended criminal penalties and a civil cause of action for acts performed as part of an ongoing criminal organization. The RICO Act focuses specifically on racketeering and allows the leaders of a syndicate to be tried for the crimes they ordered others to do or assisted them in doing, closing a perceived loophole that allowed a person who instructed someone else to, for example, murder, to be exempt from the trial because they did not actually commit the crime personally.
23. **Conspiracy:** In criminal law, a combination or confederacy between two or more persons formed for the purpose of committing, by their joint efforts, some unlawful or criminal act, or some act which is innocent in itself, but becomes unlawful when done by the concerted action of the conspirators, or for the purpose of using criminal or unlawful means to the commission of an act not in itself unlawful.

24. **Mail Fraud:** "There are two elements in mail fraud: (1) having devised or intending to devise a scheme to defraud (or to perform specified fraudulent acts), and (2) use of the mail for the purpose of executing, or attempting to execute, the scheme (or specified fraudulent acts)."

25. **False Imprisonment:** False Imprisonment: Intentionally restraining another person (whether physically or not) without the legal authority to do so; the unlawful restriction of a person's freedom of movement. If the false imprisonment goes on for an extended period of time or the perpetrator moves the victim, it may then become a kidnapping.

26. **Kidnapping:** The forcible abduction or stealing away of a man, woman, or child from their own country, and sending them into another. It is an offense punishable at the common law by fine and imprisonment. 4 Bl. Comm. 219. In American law, this word is seldom, if at all, applied to the abduction of other per- sons than children, and the intent to send them out of the country does not seem to constitute a necessary part of the offense. The term is said to include false imprisonment. 2 Bish. Crim. Law,

27. **Duress and Coercion:** Compulsion; force; duress. It may be either actual, (direct or positive.) where physical force is put upon a man to compel him to do an act against his will, or implied, (legal or constructive.) where the relation of the parties is such that one is under subjection to the other and is thereby constrained to do what his free will would refuse.

28. **Material Misrepresentation:** If known to the other party, a contract, deal, or transaction could have been aborted, or significantly altered by this deliberate hiding or falsification of a material fact.

29. **Fraudulent Misrepresentation:** Fraudulent misrepresentation occurs when a party to a contract knowingly makes an untrue statement of fact which induces the other party to enter that contract. Fraudulent misrepresentation also occurs when the party either does not believe the truth of his or her statement of fact or is reckless as regards its truth. A claimant who has been the victim of alleged fraudulent misrepresentation can claim both rescission, which will set the contract aside, and damages.

30. **Negligent Misrepresentation:** A party that is trying to induce another party

to a contract has a duty to ensure that reasonable care is taken as regards the accuracy of any representations of fact that may lead to the latter party to enter the contract. If such reasonable care to ensure the truth of a statement is not taken, then the wronged party may be the victim of negligent misrepresentation. Negligent misrepresentation can also occur in some cases when a party makes a careless statement of fact or does not have sufficient reason for believing in that statement's truth. As with fraudulent misrepresentation, claimants can pursue both damages and a rescission of the contract.

31. **Corruption:** Illegality, a vicious and fraudulent intention to evade the prohibitions of the law. The act of an official or fiduciary person who unlawfully and wrongfully uses his station or character to procure some benefit for himself or for another person, contrary to duty and the rights of others.

32. **Judicial Corruption:** This is corruption by the judiciary and or its officers.

33. **Breach of Fiduciary Trust:** Fiduciary trust is derived from the Roman law and means (as a noun) a person holding the character of a trustee, or a character analogous to

that of a trustee, in respect to the trust and confidence involved in it and the scrupulous good faith and candor which it requires. Thus, a person is a fiduciary who is invested with rights and powers to be exercised for the benefit of another person. Svanoe v. Jurgens, 144 111.507, 33 N. E. 955; Stoll v. King, 8 How. Prac. (N. Y.) 299. As an adjective it means of the nature of a trust; having the characteristics of a trust; analogous to a trust; relating to or founded upon a trust or confidence.

34. **Violations of the solemn oaths** of office required by of federal government officials.

35. **Undue influence** and unlawful menace against the American people

36. **Human Rights Denied:** Please see the UNITED NATIONS Declaration of Human Rights.

And many other crimes too numerous to list here.

RESOURCES

If you choose, you may contact the Michigan General Assembly, and they will refer you to your state assembly. They have lots of information on their website for your review. They also have weekly national informational calls that you may participate in. You may contact them at:

989-450-5522 Monday through Thursday, 2 to 7 pm EST
Thursday Night 9 pm EST call-in number: 712-770-4160,
Access Code: 226823#
Website: http://1stmichiganassembly.info
Email: contentmanager1@yahoo.com

Each state is a sovereign nation. In my case, I live in the Republic of Texas. If you live in the Texas, I encourage you to contact them for more information.

Website: www.thetexasrepublic.com
Email: reptx777@att.net
Phone: 1-888-656-5515
1-888-605-4528

Anna Von Reitz has provided some editable documents that you may fill out and record in your county court house. These documents give public notice you have changed your political status from a corporate citizen of the UNITED STATES OF AMERICA, INC., to that of a free man or woman living on the land in peace with all of your God given rights protected by our founding documents and that you now operate on American common law.

Here is the link to the basic package of editable forms by Anna Von Reitz:

http://annavonreitz.com/basicforms.pdf

To find more of Anna's work at the following link. I recommend reading Anna Von Reitz's articles and books. Go to http://www.annavonreitz.com/ for more information.

BOOKS

America: Some Assembly Required (2018)

Judge Anna von Reitz Interview: Taking Back America (2018)

Miscellaneous Writings featuring Anna von Reitz: from the Maine Republic Email Alert (2017)

"As It Is the Truth" (2016)

You Know Something is Wrong When..... An American Affidavit of Probable Cause by Anna von Reitz (2015)

Disclosure 101: What You Need to Know by Anna von Reitz (2014)

The UCC Connection: How to Free Yourself from Legal Tyranny by David E. Robinson (2013)

Give Yourself Credit: Money Doesn't Grow on Trees! By David E. Robinson (2010)

New Beginning Study Course: Connect the Dots and See by David E. Robinson (2009)

Commercial Law Applied: Learn to Play the Game by David E. Robinson (2012)

Failure to File & Conspiracy: United States vs. Messier & Robinson – No. 2:14-cr-00083-DBH by David E. Robinson (2014)

Be the One: To Execute Your Trust by David E. Robinson (2012)

Asset Protection: Pure Trust Organizations by David E. Robinson (2011)

Hardcore Redemption-in-Law: Commercial Freedom & Release by David E. Robinson (2010)

Secrets Of The U.S. Tax Code: In 10 Easy Segments by Anonymous by David E. Robinson (2017)

EDUCATIONAL LINKS

Administrating-Your-Public-Servants@GoogleGroups.com

Administrating-Your-Public-Servants@YahooGroups.com

www.sovereigntyinternational.fyi

http://sovereigntyinternational.wordpress.com

https://steemit.com/@sovereigntyintl

https://www.youtube.com/user/sovereignliving

www.thetexasrepublic.com

https://www.youarelaw.org/

www.HowToWinInCourt.com?refercode=BM0063

youarelaw.org

CPSIA information can be obtained
at www.ICGtesting.com
Printed in the USA
LVHW091412160919
631218LV00015B/757/P